THE COMPLETE VIZSLA

GAY GOTTLIEB

New York

HOWELL BOOK HOUSE
A Simon & Schuster Macmillan company,
1633 Broadway, New York, NY 10019.

MACMILLAN is a registered trademark of Macmillan, Inc.

Library of Congress Cataloging-in-Publication data

Gottlieb, Gay.
  The complete Vizsla / Gay Gottlieb.

      p.   cm.
    ISBN 0-87605-377-0
    1. Vizsla.   I. Title.

  SF429.V5G67   1992
  636.7'52 – dc20

92-3399
CIP

10 9 8 7 6 5 4
Printed and bound in Singapore

ACKNOWLEDGEMENTS

I wish to thank all the photographers for their generous contributions. Also, to so many in the breed in Britain and abroad who unstintingly gave me information and invaluable material. My gratitude to my new-found friends in America, Lynn Worth and Chauncey Smith, who so promptly and enthusiastically sent me all the material I asked for concerning the breed in their country.

Gay Gottlieb with her Hungarian Vizslas.   *S. Hart*

CONTENTS

Part of a Gothic panel (15th century) from the Christian Museum in Esztergom, Hungary, showing a dog believed to be a Vizsla.

Chapter One

ORIGINS

THE HUNGARIAN VIZSLA IN BRITAIN

Before the Second World War the sport of game shooting in Britain was confined mainly to wealthy land owners and to the aristocracy who owned large estates. On the driven shoots all types of gundogs were used, each for a specific purpose: pointers to point, retrievers to retrieve, and spaniels to hunt cover. After the war, customs and circumstances changed, both socially and economically, causing the pattern of shooting to alter. Many large estate owners were forced to break up their land to solve financial difficulties. Finance, not status, controlled who could afford to shoot. Small shooting syndicates were formed, so that the expense of stocking and running a shoot could be shared. Many enthusiasts preferred shooting over their own dogs, so they required a different type of gundog, and shooters came to realise that the all-round versatile continental breeds suited their purpose very well. What better than a dog who had the potential to do the work of three specialists all rolled into one? It was in this context that the HPRs – hunt, point and retrieve breeds – came into their own. The Hungarian Vizsla is classified by the Kennel Club in this group of gundogs. Purists on the shooting scene argue that the specialist gundogs do a particular job with excellence and that the HPRs are jack of all trades and master of none. However, for the shooter who wants to take his dog to hunt, point game, flush, mark the fall and retrieve, there is no more willing companion. An enthusiastic convert writes of the Vizsla:-

"To see him quartering the ground into the wind in front of a line of guns is a pure delight. He is never out of range and he whips on to point when his nose tells him there is game ahead. He will remain on point until told to flush, he will sit to order until told to retrieve. His retrieving ability is unsurpassed because his phenomenal nose is as sure to find dead game as it is to point the covey of partridge. When following a runner he will go nose to the ground, but when he is quartering to locate game he holds his nose high for air scent, such is his instinct. When his master takes him on a formal shoot in a Labrador role he will sit steady as rock marking the fall of birds until sent to retrieve. When taken alone by his master pottering on a rough shoot he is a real bag-filler; he can do anything a Labrador, a Pointer or a Springer can do."

Praise indeed for the golden hunting dog! It is safe to say that once the art of training this breed has been mastered – this "many-sided hunting dog", as the Hungarians describe the breed – few return to the long-established gundog breeds, and the number of enthusiasts increases every season.

THE VIZSLA'S ORIGINS

What is it that has given the Vizsla its fine instincts and stature? How did this multi-purpose dog first arrive on the scene? Its evolution is shrouded in mystery and the passage of time. It is reputedly of very ancient origin. It is said to have descended from the hunting dogs brought into the Carpathian mountain region by the migrating Magyars in the ninth century. During the Turkish occupation of this territory lasting 150 years, these dogs were freely bred with the Yellow Turkish dogs and other breeds. By the sixteenth century the name Vizsla seems to have been in common usage. In the eighteenth and nineteenth century this dog became the Vizsla we know and see today. It was in the hands of clever and knowledgeable breeders, who were in pursuit of a high performance of excellence in the field. They were dedicated to the correct development, adding other bloodlines to that of the native Vizsla to strengthen the characteristics as they became evident. This list of breeds thought to have been used lengthens as time goes on. For pointing ability, the Irish and English Setters were introduced; for hunting and scenting, the Bloodhound, the German Vorsthund, the Balkan Beagle, the ancient Foxhound, the Pammion Hound and Romanian Copie were used. The Greyhound is mentioned, and now research indicates that the Sloughi was an ancestor. Shooting parties with their keepers came over from Britain, Germany, Austria and Bohemia, bringing their hunting dogs with them, and these dogs are also said to have contributed to the gene pool. The origin of the breed bears some similarity to that from which the hound strain developed. The name 'hound' was given to the dogs who hunted by scent. In the Vizsla, the hound-like features – excess dewlap, throatiness, drooping eyes, and a heavy gait – were not desirable. But the excellent knowledgeable nose – the most desirable trait – has been retained. The Pointer qualities – the deep chest, good running ability, and an effortless, graceful stride – more closely align themselves with those typifying the Vizsla today in every country.

In the twenties, when Hungary was robbed of so much of her territory, a movement was

'Witti' owned by Gyula Popovich in Hungary. This dog's name appears in every pedigree dated 1918. For sixteen years his puppies were in-bred and those with white were culled. *Nimrod 1918.*

initiated to save the breed from extinction. This effort gained support, and Count Laszlo Esterhazy, Dr Kalman Polgar, Elmer Petocz, Captain Baba, and others, founded the Oriszagos Vizsla Club in 1924. This date marks the beginning of the history of the modern Vizsla. Prior to this, no Vizsla had been registered. The founders of the club searched out and registered a few Vizslas with the most desirable characteristics, and a tightly controlled breeding programme was formulated. A Breed Standard was worked out in order to achieve the strain and type of dog they were looking for. Most of the dogs they chose were owned by the founders and friends, it is reported. Three stud dogs were said to be accepted, Ripp, Witti and Treff, and three bitches, Lidi, Kati and Boresa. There were many faults to be eliminated. The breed had too much white, it had light eyes and the wrong coat colour. The feet and pasterns were incorrect, and in many specimens the muzzle was too short and snipey. In the early photographs many Hungarian dogs had some degree of white on the chest and feet.

Thus a handful of enthusiasts regenerated the breed in Hungary. In 1944, it is said that

Karoly Thuroczy with his Vizsla 'Trick.' Nimrod 1917.

'Hanved': In the early photos many Hungarian dogs had some degree of white on the chest and feet.
          Nimrod 1917.

Martai Lurko – the treasured golden hunting dog – his name appears in many pedigrees today.

5,000 Vizslas were registered. Before any stock was allowed to be registered it had to be shown, in order to achieve a certain status. To me, this demonstrates the ideals and principles of showing. It is fascinating to realise that although our gene pools must be different today in every country, if we were able to look at our extended pedigrees together, we would find the same few names from which our stock originated.

TWO WORLD WARS AND THE RUSSIAN OCCUPATION

After two World Wars and the Russian occupation, the Hungarian Empire was diminished, and much of the territory was divided between Romania, Austria, Czechoslavakia and Yugoslavia. It is claimed that ninety per cent of Vizslas were destroyed during the Russian occupation. Many Hungarians fled the country, smuggling their dogs out with them, and so the breed became established in Europe and further afield. Many members of the British and American military commissions brought dogs home with them. Until this time, the Vizsla had been confined to Hungary, jealously treasured and protected for many centuries, controlled and guarded by the Hungarian nobility, who were adamant that this breed should not leave the country. However, their treasured golden hunting dog finally came to be appreciated far and wide.

THE WORKING VIZSLA IN HUNGARY

The Vizsla was used originally to scent and search for birds, which were either netted or caught by falcons, before firearms were introduced in the 1700s. This sleek, short-haired, rusty-gold Pointer adapted readily to the shotgun when that became the nobility's preferred method of hunting game birds. These dogs were highly valued for their all-round versatility, enabling them to work on the plains of Hungary, which were largely agricultural and rich in game. They were bred to work on fur or feather, to be fast, and to possess a good nose that would permit them to find game in thick cover, in crops and high grasslands, or in the immense areas of corn. They were called to work upon the giant hare, to put up quail, woodcock and pheasant, flush water fowl and wild duck, and goose. They also had to track and hold deer, wild boar and wolf, with several dogs working together. They flourished under these conditions, tolerating extremes of climate – hot dry summers and bitterly cold winters. The Vizsla proves this today, thriving all over Europe, Australia, America, South Africa and of course Great Britain, where it has to deal with heat, cold, rain or wind, frost and snow.

THE WORKING HUNGARIAN VIZSLA IN BRITAIN

The Hungarian Vizsla was introduced to Britain in 1953. The pioneers were mostly dedicated to working and breeding it as a gundog – none of the early imports came in as show dogs. Bench shows in Hungary were thought to be detrimental to the breed at this time, a view shared by most of the early fanatics in Britain, and this view is still held by many in the field today. The Hungarian Vizsla adapted easily to the British hunting scene in a variety of roles:
"On the hills it's deer."
"On the moors it's grouse."
"On the field it's all types of bird."
"On the water it's duck."
                                        D. Ryan

A fully trained dog could be up on the grouse moors early in the season; later on it may accompany its owner to work on driven partridge, duck or pheasant; and then engage in some rough shooting on rabbit, pigeon or hare. It might have to work roots, stubble and plough, grass and heathland, light woodlands, ditches and hedgerow, some dense with briar and nettle. It is an excellent dog in water, willing to work river banks, marshlands or wetlands. It has been found to be an asset for stalking and tracking deer.

The working Vizsla in Hungary is called upon to retrieve Woodcock...

...Pheasant...

...Wild duck.

Tracking and holding wild deer.

Tracking and holding wild boar.   *All pictures taken in Hungary.*

The Vizsla in America is appreciated for its outstanding nose.
D. C. Metto-N-Futaki's Rapstone Red SH.

It adapts particularly well to the ancient sport of falconry, which is increasingly popular in Britain. Dog and bird work in unison. The Vizsla must hunt, point and be steady to flush; its trustworthiness is essential, its retrieving instincts must be curbed. This same dog will retrieve game on command, if carefully trained. Wild fowling is a cold, wet sport, and the dog may be required to sit in water for long periods – not ideal for the short-coated HPRs, but the Vizsla acquits itself well in duck flighting or wild fowling on the foreshore. Its pointing ability is appreciated when grouse counting, and its soft mouth is valued when egg collecting. In the competitive stakes more owners are field trialing their Vizslas, and many are now winning awards at working tests.

THE WORKING VIZSLA IN AMERICA

Where does the Vizsla fit into the American hunting and shooting scene? There is scope for many kinds of work for the HPRs in this vast country. There is a need for very wide ranging horizon hunters, for close working quartering dogs, and for dogs somewhere in between. These dogs may be used with shooters on horseback ranging open prairie, or gentle, rolling countryside, providing a variety of hunting conditions, such as plantations of small cedar and pine trees with creeks running through, bean and cornfields with grassy swales, or on driven walking shoots, where rough shooting dogs are required. The dogs must work fast

The Vizsla is a 'quail dog': Willo Runn's Metto Megan, pictured at four months old.

and hard, and far out, swerving into a strong point; the bird is up and shot in a matter of seconds with the dogs still forward. More birds are put up and shot as the dogs move on, still running. They are ideal for grouse and woodcock or pheasant, where the Vizsla needs to be medium ranging. A close-hunting Vizsla is required for the mid-western quail hunter too; the shooter who hunts on small plots of privately owned land would find a big-going covey dog would get its owner into trouble too often with landowners. The Vizsla in America is also appreciated for its outstanding nose: a quail dog must be able to pick up the slight traces of scent wafting up from scattered birds. The Vizsla has typically all the olfactory equipment needed to nail every bird in the vicinity of its walking handler.

There seems to be a fundamental difference in the way British and American handlers work their dogs. The shooters require their dog to hunt and point, but the British Vizsla has to flush the bird and be steady to shot – its whole training is based on absolute steadiness to flush – whereas in America the handler gets up to the dog on point, and flushes the bird himself. I would suggest that British dogs are not so hard going because of the absolute necessity for steadiness; the handler, in many circumstances, works his dogs at a distance, and does not expect to be close to the dog, unless it is called in. Chauncey Smith, who trained with, and eventually took over the famous Futaki prefix of Count Bela Hadik from Hungary, has trained many Vizslas. These have included the first AKC Vizsla dual Champion, and the first AKC dual Champion bitch. He writes: "Steadiness to wing and shot is the difference between a really polished performance and often a mediocre one. Over the years at the Verbank Hunting Fishing Club most of our members shot a large percentage of their birds – and most of them do not have dogs that are steady to wing and shot. I see nothing wrong with breaking on shot in a real hunting situation. Steadiness to wing and shot demonstrates the trainability of a dog. I think this is an important component of a good gundog. If you cannot train a dog for your particular purpose, it does not say much for the dog. I think it is absolutely fantastic that British dogs have to "Hup" on flush, as Retrievers and Spaniels do in the USA."

It would seem that we all understand the Vizsla temperament well enough to accept that it demands time in training. Its complex personality and way of working needs enlightened handling. Its wide repertoire takes time to develop, and if we are to make the best use of its all-round performance, it is vital that it is seen as different from the specialist breeds and other HPRs, for they are all unique. The Vizsla poses a challenge to the trainer, but with dedicated support and informed awareness of the breed's characteristics, many have proved that its performance in the field can be the highest.

Chauncey Smith describes the Vizsla as a "walking gentleman's shooting dog," using the word 'gentleman' to describe the nature of the hunter. He explained this belief in an article:

"Generally speaking, the closer you become to a Vizsla, the more you lead him into doing what you want, and the more you show your appreciation for his efforts, the better dog you will have. If you are a rough and tumble trainer this breed just isn't for you. If you have little patience or a quick temper, ditto. Even if you are a reasonable, gentle person, but one who cannot take the trouble to praise your dog for his good work, you may have some problems.

Chauncey Smith with enthusiastic young Vizsla pups.

The Vizsla wants to be a respected colleague, and the only way you can communicate that status to his mind is through frequent praise and petting. As soon as he understands that he can please his boss, he will die working for him. Force breaking or electric collars are not for him."

Chauncey goes on to describe the present situation for working Vizslas in the USA. "Less than a third of Vizslas are run in Field Trials. The breed is really split, as in most sporting breeds in the USA, and in many parts of the world, in fact. But with a little luck maybe the hunting tests introduced by the AKC will help, and with more people competing this will encourage the development of the natural instincts of Vizslas. The idea is that some people will go on to Field Trial their dogs, at least then we can see if the dogs have some natural ability. The show people want the dog to be little and close, as far as I am concerned, but still, it is a step forward. Most people in the USA that run Vizslas who do not compete in

Field Trials, feel very intimidated by the professionals and the horseback handling, and some believe that the Vizsla should not be anything but a walking-shooting dog. But I feel that the Field Trials are one of the most important yardsticks that we have to pick the best breeding stock. For if you do not breed dogs with a lot of desire, you end up with a mediocre bird dog."

Chauncey believes the pendulum will start swinging back in the direction of the medium-ranging hunting dog, because there is no territory now for the wide-ranging, hard-running dogs: so that is the Vizsla of the future. He also believes there will be very few horseback handling Field Trials. He states: "The problem I see with horseback handling is not that horseback handling is not good, but it is abused. The horse is supposed to be used as a conveyance only. But the judges up in the saddle have allowed the handlers on horseback to use the course as a horse race, and to use the horse as a training aide."

Chapter Two

THE BREED DEVELOPS

EARLY YEARS IN BRITAIN

As we have seen, all Vizslas in the world today can be traced back to a common ancestry. There are variations in size, shape and colour in the Vizsla breed and these are not only the result of different Breed Standards in use, but nature and nurture play a big part. It is interesting to note that the British and American pedigrees share Hungarian and Czechoslovakian lines. Photographs of dogs from these two countries clearly show that although the type remains the same, the conformation differs somewhat. The Hungarian dogs appear lighter in bone and smaller in stature, the Czech dogs are heavier with a good deal of substance. This difference was noticeable in some of our basic stock. Today the Vizsla is more uniform, accepting that each kennel has its own type, but basically the general bone structure and quality conforms to the Breed Standard. More of our Vizslas are placed in the Championship Gundog Groups these days, proving they are competing successfully against the other gundog breeds.

First two imports

Significant imports have played an essential part in making the breed in Britain what it is today. Ten Vizslas came from the country of origin and five from the United States. Others have come in from France, Austria and Holland. The first Vizslas to be registered came into Britain in 1953. Mr and Mrs J. Wyndham-Harris returned from Hungary bringing back their family companions, Ernest and Agnes, who were brother and sister. Between them they

Matai Dugo, bred by M. Farkashazi. Note the undocked tail.

The Maygar Vizsla.

Sh. Ch. Futaki Lazslo: the third USA import in 1973.					*Pearce.*

produced three litters. Five puppies from one of the litters and two from another were exported to Charles Hunt in America. Major Petty, in turn, went to Charles Hunt and imported a bitch, Adalyn Von Hunt, to Britain, thus setting up the well known Strawbridge prefix in 1955. Several puppies from Adalyn's litters were put back to the Strawbridge line and exported to America. Agnes and Adalyn, whose sire and dam were Czech, produced thirty-six puppies between them, and so we can see how closely linked British basic stock is to Hungarian, Czech and American lines.

Second USA Import

The second USA import, Warhorse Lwow, came into Britain in 1970. He came in with the Henderson family as a companion dog. He had a very fine pedigree: his grandsire was Ch. Miclos Shloss Loosdorf, one of the top sires of his day, and the first Show Champion in America. 'Horse' sired two litters, his offspring contributing significantly to the success of the Abbeystag, Galfrid and Russetmantle prefixes.

Austrian import Bingo Vom Wurmbrandpark.   *Owned by L. Petrie Hay.*

Third USA Import

The third USA import, Sh. Ch. Futaki Lazslo, was brought into Britain in 1972 by Mr and Mrs J. Gray (Abbeystag prefix), and he featured significantly in the breed's progress. The Futaki line was founded by Bela Hadik, one of the most serious and successful breeders in the early days of the breed in America. Bela Hadik believed passionately in the dual-purpose dog for bench and field, and it was he who bred the first American dual Champion, Futaki Daroz, as well as many bench Champions, field Champions and three of the four dual Champions in the USA. Bela Hadik was born in Budapest in 1905; he left in 1945, after serving in the Hungarian cavalry in World War II, to live in America. He died in 1971, but his prefix lives on, perpetuated by the well known Chauncey Smith, who bred and exported Lazslo. This dog became a Show Champion himself, and his line has produced directly five Champions, and several Show Champions.

*Mocsarkeresco Vac Of Galfrid; imported from Hungary by A. Boys. Bred by Kiss
Itsuam in 1976.*   *Pearce.*

Other significant imports

Alec Macrae, in Scotland, was one of the first to train his Vizslas to field trial standard. In
1956 he imported Tandorsi Gyongy from Hungary, and she features in most of today's
pedigrees. She was followed by Sibriktelepi Tigi, and when she was mated to Anya, the
Kinford prefix was founded. Kinford Vlada joined the Waidman kennels, owned by Major
and Mrs W. Petrie-Hay, and Vlada was dam to the first two Show Champions in the breed,
Sh. Ch. Waidman Remus and Sh. Ch. Waidman Zuszie. Bingo Vom Wurmbrandpark and
Bella Vom Wurmbrandpark were two Austrian imports in the Waidman kennel, and both
contributed significantly to the breed. Waidman Brok, son of Bella, probably did more to
contribute to the success of Vizslas in the field and field trials than any other dog in the
breed.

    Evan Young in Scotland worked his Tintohill Vizslas on the grouse moors, and he bred
Tintohill Astra, who was the foundation bitch to Mrs Kathleen Auchterlonie's Saline prefix.
She imported Szeppataki Csaba from Hungary; he also figures in many successful working
and showing lines. The Saline Vizslas were worked regularly, and figured frequently in field
trial awards. Angela Boys imported Matai Sari Of Galfrid, in whelp to Matai Lurko, in 1972,
and also Farad-Putztai Charlotte Of Galfrid in the same year, giving British pedigrees more
important working lines.

Later, two more Matai Vizslas were imported from Hungary: Matai Vica and Matai Pirok, and both featured successfully in the field trialing scene. From 1977 to 1990 one more Hungarian came over to the Galfrid kennels, Mocsarkeresco Vac Of Galfrid. These all contributed to the gene pool, introducing valuable direct Hungarian lines.

Formation of the Club and Society

Christmas greetings sent by Evan Young to all Vizsla owners in America in the *Vizsla News* read: "Greetings from Vizslas in Scotland to their cousins across the seas. Mrs Petrie-Hay is trying to get a Vizsla club started over here. We really need one to get all the owners acquainted with the breed and also for the people to meet. A club would be able to get the breed better known by running club trials and shows. We had a good shooting season, a big blizzard drove the grouse to the lower grounds in huge packs, saw over 500 sitting well out on the mow and were very wild."

The Hungarian Vizsla Club's first AGM was held in 1968, and with the development of the breed, the Hungarian Vizsla Society and the Hungarian Vizsla Club are now well established. Both foster the good of the breed, aiming to help newcomers in every aspect. Each organises open shows and their own trials and Championship shows. Both put on working tests, and the Society holds novice to qualifying open stakes, and spring pointing tests. There are also tuition days and fun days, all encouraging novices to have a go. In 1990 the Society introduced a new voluntary code of ethics for members; this is significant, demonstrating that with the increase in numbers and breeders, inevitably, undesirable practices come about. This code was especially drawn up to encourage quality not quantity of litters bred, thus endeavouring to hold breeders and stud dog owners responsible for their actions. The breed continues to be relatively small in Britain and is valued highly. Annual registrations are approximately 220.

Code of Ethics

1. Members will consider the welfare of their dogs and the breed above any personal gain or profit and will take responsibility for any dogs they own.
2. Members will only breed from Hungarian Vizslas of sound temperament, which show natural ability, and will always strive to produce Hungarian Vizslas conforming to the standard as published by The Kennel Club.
3. Members will not knowingly allow their stud dogs to serve bitches of less than two years of age or over the age of seven. Neither dogs nor bitches in poor health, of unsound temperament or with any serious hereditary disease will be used for breeding.
4. Stud dog owners will use their discretion as to the number and suitability of bitches covered each year.
5. Members will not allow their bitches to whelp more than once in every twelve months or before two years of age or over the age of seven.

6. Members shall ensure that any stock from which they breed shall be registered with The Kennel Club, in accordance with the rules in force at the time.

7. Members will not, when advertising, knowingly misrepresent themselves or their stock, and will deal only in an open and honest manner with clients who shall be advised of any fault the dog may have. Clients buying stock shall be encouraged to present the dog to a veterinary surgeon within three days of purchase. Should a veterinary surgeon, at such an examination, advise that the dog is not in good health, members will verify this opinion and, if necessary, take back such a dog and refund the purchase price.

8. Members will be encouraged to take advantage of any relevant official scheme devised to test a dog's soundness.

9. Members will, when engaged in competitive events with their dogs, conduct themselves in such a way as not to bring discredit to the breed or the Society, and will demonstrate good sportsmanship at all times.

EARLY YEARS IN AMERICA

First imports

In the thirties Queen Elima of Italy was given two Vizslas; Pope Pius XII also owned the breed for many years. Prince Rainier of Monaco's father owned two, both of whom showed excellence, in the ring and in the field respectively. H.R.H. Antoinette of Monaco has been the patron of the Hungarian Vizsla Club in Britain for several years; she has been devoted to the breed since childhood.

The first known Vizsla arrived in the USA in 1938. Joseph Pulltzer of St. Louis gave his sister a dog, Zsoka Of Sashegy, which he bought from Baron Michaly Kendes in Hungary. In l950 Frank Tallman was given a bitch called Sari, and she was the first bitch to be shown in the United States. The bitch and her two puppies were obtained from a Hungarian refugee. Tallman also imported a dog, Rex Del Gelsimo, from Italy, and a strong line was established in the Mid-West, by mating him to Sari. It was also in the fifties that Colonel Jemo Dus, Director of the Vizsla Club in Hungary, arrived in America. He brought two of his favourite Vizslas with him, Kati and Judka, smuggling them through Russian-occupied Hungary. Also in the fifties, Jack Hatfield and William Olson imported a total of fourteen Vizslas from Germany and Austria, including two, Gelse and Gemme Von Schloss Loosdorf, who figure in many pedigrees. The breed was beginning to make it in the ring at this time too, exhibited in the Miscellaneous classes.

The early Vizsla importers and breeders in the USA had difficulty in obtaining complete pedigrees. This was due to the chaos of World War II and its aftermath. Many owners fled from Hungary, losing certificates and records in most cases. The National Kennel Club created confusion due to political unrest, restraints and internal politics. However, tracing back the early days of the Vizsla's introduction to the United States, the vastness of the country compared to Britain is so impressive, and the way the breed took off is equally so.

Sari: the first bitch to be shown in the United States.

The British imports to date are twenty-one; I hesitate to attempt to count the USA imports, but it is fascinating to realise that despite the difference in numbers, all our dogs share the same few ancestors. There was much groundwork to be done before the breed could be well and truly established in America. After the first few Vizslas arrived, Frank Tallman, amongst others, worked ceaselessly for years to gain recognition for the breed from the Kennel Club and the American Field. Eventually in 1953, the breed owners organised the Magyar Vizsla Club of America, with Frank Tallman as president. The term 'Vizsla' was adopted as in Hungary, whereas in Britain we still use the term 'Hungarian Vizsla' for this golden pointer.

In 1960 the Vizsla was officially recognised by the American Kennel Club. A total of five hundred dogs had to be submitted with three-generation pedigrees, although some were accepted with incomplete pedigrees. It was through the efforts of Charles Hunt that this was achieved. By 1983, 1,859 dogs were registered. When the first imports arrived in Britain in 1953, we had little or no trouble registering them, and few of us realise how fortunate we were that most of the groundwork had been done. The official voice of the Vizsla Club of America is the *Vizsla News*. In the impressive 'decade of Vizslas', 1960-1970, A. Lucas, president, writes: "Competition is the best way to prove superiority and breeding improvement. The greatest Vizsla bred served his master well as a fine companion and hunting dog, but through no fault of his own never served the breed."

The Vizsla, Friend, Companion and Gundog

(Written for the revised version of the 1986 American Breed Standard)

"The Vizsla, added to the ranks of the American Kennel Club in 1960, is a distinctively different dog. It fills the need for a one-dog owner who desires a friendly dog and a hunting companion. The Vizsla is a 365-days-a-year dog, accepting the role of protector, friend and hunter, and expecting the degree of respect and rank clearly higher than that of 'a dog'.

"After surviving countless wars and centuries of limited and selective breeding, the Vizsla was re-bred from near extinction and combines the finest in beauty, character and hunting ability with a strong desire to please. He is lightweight and agile, running with effortless grace.

"Now on the American scene and other countries beside its native land, he should never be allowed to become less than a 'true Vizsla' or different from the dog that still represents the National Dog of Hungary.

"The Vizsla should remain true to type whether in the show ring, field or at home with the family, representing all physical characteristics which have distinguished him for centuries: the unique and coveted Magyar Vizsla. The Vizsla Standard describing this breed to Americans is but an abbreviated form, and can give only a meager representation of the Vizsla. The *Vizsla News* carries articles from many areas including Hungary on show standards, and subsequent articles by individuals clarifying the many facets that combine to characterize the true Vizsla. Well-rounded perfection, in anything, is a complex and detailed study. Only by knowing the standard and then by breeding, training, trialing and showing the Vizsla, can the breed be preserved and perpetrated in its 'true type'. Membership of owners and breeders is needed in the National breed club to secure a truly dedicated group of people interested in maintaining the breed and assuring proper management for it here in America.

"The Vizsla deserves good owners, trainers and judges so that future generations may also enjoy the noble characteristics of this classy sporting dog. Vizsla breeders – that is, all people who own a Vizsla and allow it to be used at stud or whelp even one litter of puppies – should first learn the magnitude of the breed, and use only fully registered (both AKC and FD SB) stock that is well within the standard in physical appearance – bold and birdy hunters in the field, and personable companions in the home. Vizslas should be selected for all their good qualities, not just one; however, good and bad characteristics are passed on to the offspring, so one fault in either sex can be a sufficient reason not to consider it for breeding. Owners of Vizslas should never breed for "just puppies" but always for the improvement of the breed. The Vizsla, in these modern and rapidly changing times, is under no handicap; accepting it easily in their stride, maintaining their love of the wide open fields and the whirr and flutter of wings, and striving always to please their master. A Vizsla owner soon finds that he has found a whole new world through the eyes of his noble friend ... and that they share heart and soul."

Ch. Fleckes Of Sageacre, a son of Ch. Sandor Von Debretsin.
Owned and bred by Connie Johnson of the famous Sageacre prefix.   Bennett Assoc.

Ch. Miclos Schloss Loosdorf – "The Count" – the first Champion in the breed, in 1960. Owned by Harry Warholm. Bred by Weiss Jensen.

Ch. Futaki Darocz: the first dual Champion, made up in 1965. Owned and bred by Bela Hadik. Handled to finish by Chauncey Smith.

Dual Ch. Szekeres Kis Szereto: the first Vizsla bitch to become a dual Champion. Owned by Carole Smith. Bred by J. and P. Carter.

There have been many great Vizslas over the decades. During the sixties and seventies there were stud dogs producing several Champions. Ch. Sandor Von Debretsin, owned by Mr and Mrs A. Carpenter, sired sixteen Champions; including the highly successful Ch. Fleckes Of Sageacre; Ch. Puerco Pete Barat sired fifteen Champions; Am. Can. Field Ch. Ripp Barat sired eleven Champions, and his name appears in many pedigrees. He was campaigned by Paul Sabo and bred by Dr Osborn. Ch. Miclos Schloss Loosdorf ("The Count"), owned by Harry Warholm and bred by Weiss Jensen was the first Champion in the breed, in 1960; he had fifty Best of Breeds, and many Group placings. He was the top winning Vizsla in 1961-1962, and it is said that he was never defeated by another male Vizsla. He produced ten Champions and appears in the pedigrees of many of the top Show and Field Vizslas. He also appears in many British pedigrees. Ch. Duchess Of Shirob was the first Vizsla bitch to gain her title, in 1960. She was "The Count's" dam. The first Field Champion came in 1965 and that was Field Ch. Brokselle, owned by D. Anderson and bred by Dr Osborn. Ch. Gypsy's Bronze Bomber won the first Vizsla Specialty Show and took the first Group win in the breed. Ch. Piros Of Mile High, owned by A. Debarr and bred by R. Holcomb was the first Vizsla to win Best in Show.

*Triple Ch.
Cariads Kutya
Kai Costa.
Owned by the
Costas. Bred by
Marion Coffman
and Linda
Greenfield.*

*The Nationals 1990 was a 'family affair'. Pictured left to right: Dual and AFCh.
Riverbend Deacons Dandy (first in Field Trial class), sire of: Ch. Oakleaf's Dandy
Dalton (Best of Breed), Kisadee's El Casador (Best of Winners) and Oakleaf's Ever
When Chances R (Reserve Winners Dog).   Downey.*

Ch. Harrann's Tulipann VCA winning the 1985 Specialty from the Veterans Bitch class. She was in the 1991 Parade of Champions. Bernard W. Kernnan.

The first dual Champion in the breed was Ch. Futaki Darocz, made up in 1965. He was owned and bred by Bela Hadik and handled to finish by Chauncey Smith. The first Vizsla bitch to become a dual Champion was Dual Ch. Szekeres Kis Szereto, a daughter of Ch. Futaki Darocz. She was owned by Carole Smith and bred by J. and P. Carter.

By the mid seventies the HVA recognised that the Vizsla was being divided into two separate breeds – the Field and the Show dog. The 'field trialers' were said to be at odds with the 'show people'. The result was the idea of the Specialties, and in 1976 the first national event, combining conformation, Field and Obedience took place. There were fourteen Obedience entries, compared with a figure of fifty-six in 1991. It became clear that a good-looking dog could hunt well, and a good hunting dog could also be of decent conformation. This was proved by Ch. Cariads Kutya Kai Costa, owned by the Costas and bred by Marion Coffman and Linda Greenfield, the first triple Champion, gaining this honoured title after competing in the show ring, the Field, and at Obedience trials.

The Vizsla Club of America's National Specialty was a family affair in 1990. Dual and AFC Riverbend Deacons Dandy came first in the Field Trial class. He was the sire of Ch. Oakleaf's Dandy Dalton, Best of Breed, Kiskadee's El Casador, Best of Winners, and of

Ch. Lyons Skipjack Of Harrann: 1991 VCA Best of Breed winner. Owned by William and Joy Lyons.

Oakleaf's Ever When Chances R, Reserve Winners Dog. The entry at the 1991 National Specialty Show was up to 274 Vizslas, a new record by some distance. Dr Bernard McGivern, judge, breeder and handler, involved in the breed for thirty years, describes the line-up: "What a sight! Seventy-five Vizsla Champions, most of who were multiple Group placing Vizsla and Best in Show winners, entering a ring the size of a basketball court. This is the largest assembly of Champion Vizslas ever seen. Those at the ringside who were not exhibiting, stood in absolute awe, and the flashes from cameras reminded one of a Presidential Press conference. I felt enormously honoured to have a dog in the presence of

Ch. Triads XXVI Karat Oakleaf: 1991 Field Championship winner. Owned by K. Pullen and J. Bunk. Bred by Linda Kelly.

this assemblage!" At this show there was also a sixty-two Vizsla Parade of Champions, where everyone was given a chance to see the best – young and old – of what breeders had produced in the last twelve years. Ch. Lyons Skipjack Of Harann, owned by W. and J. Lyons and bred by A. Deheny and C. Spaulding, was the Best of Breed winner at the National Specialty, and Ch. Triads XXVI Karat Oakleaf, owned by K. Pullen and J. Bunk and bred by Linda Kelly, was the Field Championship winner. Ch. Russet Leather Caveat Calla was the top show dog in 1990 and 1991, and placed in the Sporting Group 111 at Westminster 1991. The Calla's owners write: "Wow, what a thrill! Best of Breed and Group 111; we are honoured to join the ranks of the great Vizslas who have won for the breed at the Garden."

In the nineties the future of American Vizslas seemed threatened not by numbers decreasing, but by out-crossing to orange or yellow Pointers. Some Field Triallers felt that by going back to headquarters, an infusion of new blood by out-crossing would produce more run. May Carpenter writes: "I have been involved with Vizslas since 1955. Twenty years later Vizsla breeders all over the world have heard of the alleged cross breeding in the USA, and it is a sad day for old-timers in the breed who have tried to do the best they could for these fabulous dogs. We have worried about size, colour, hip dysplasia, hunting ability, trainability, and made great strides on all counts. Fortunately for this wonderful breed, a concerned group of true Vizsla lovers has taken action. Hopefully everyone can work together toward what must be a common goal – protecting the pure-bred Vizsla – and this is why the Maygar Vizsla Society has been formed. It is hoped the breed will be guaranteed for future enthusiasts, and so that no breeder may be wrongfully accused of out-crossing; all AKC registered Vizslas will also be DNA fingerprint certified.

Ch. Joshua Melto: twice winner of VCA National Specialty.

Ch. Russet Leather Caveat Calla: top show dog in 1990 and 1991.
Owned by Rust and D. Jones-Ball. Bred by B. and A. Watson.

"For all US breed enthusiasts we can join together in our admiration for a certain Vizsla, owned by a heart attack patient, who upon recovering trained his dog as a Search and Rescue dog, in addition to earning Show, Obedience and Tracking titles. This dog rescued people lost in the woods, and victims of the Puerto Rican mudslides. What better kind of ambassador of the breed could we have!"

THE VIZSLA IN BRITAIN

The breed in Britain is still numerically small; for instance, it does not compare with the number of German short-haired Pointers. Some twenty years after the breed's recognition by the Kennel Club, Challenge Certificates were finally awarded in 1971. In 1991 there were sixty-five Show Champions in the breed, thirteen of which are full Champions, proving that they have attained the standard in the ring and have proved themselves in the field as well.

Sh. Ch. Waidman Remus: the first dog Show Champion in the breed. Bred by L. Petrie Hay.   Cooke.

Sh. Ch. Kinsford Zsuzsie: Britain's first Show Champion. Owned by the Fosters. Bred by L. Petrie Hay.   Pearce.

Today most successful prefixes are producing working stock as well as good-looking dogs. Of course, there are some dogs who conform to the Breed Standard and do not have the capability in the field, and some working dogs who do not make it in the ring, but it can be stated without question that the instinct to work and the characteristics are well and truly there. The Vizsla today in Britain is what it has always been in its country of origin, and the gene pool is well and truly stocked with good-looking dogs who can work. This can be proved by many of the dogs who may not make it to the top in the ring, but nevertheless, they will be in the cards one day – and these same dogs may compete in a working test, field trial or earn their living beating or picking up, or are shot over the following day.

I also believe the quality of the top dogs in the early days would hold its own today. There may not have been the quantity in the classes but the competition was high in quality. Many new dogs and prefixes grace the show ring and are in the field. Today it is not possible to know how they will influence the breed or whether they will become a force to be reckoned with. A review of past breeders and owners indicates that quite a few have come into the

Ch. Abbeystag Emilio: sire of six Show Champions, three of which became full Champions. Owned and bred by S. Gray. *Fall.*

breed and are then gone without trace. In the seventies the average entry at Championship level was between twenty and thirty. Sh. Ch. Kinsford Zsuzsie, owned by the Fosters and bred by L. Petrie Hay, won six CCs and became the first Show Champion in Great Britain in 1971. (The title 'Show Champion' is given to dogs who achieve honours in the ring, and the title 'Champion' is given to those who gain honours in the field). Zsuzsie was a great ambassadress for the breed. Sh. Ch. Waidman Remus, winner of thirteen CCs became the first dog show champion in the breed. He was bred by L. Petrie Hay and was the foundation of the Russetmantle prefix. Ch. Abbeystag Emilio, winner of six CCs, made an impact on the breed, siring six Show Champions, three of which became full Champions. His sire was imported from the United States, Sh. Ch. Futaki Lazslo, owned and bred by S. Gray.

In the eighties and early nineties the entry at a Championship show had reached an average of sixty. Ch. Russetmantle Troy, winner of thirteen CCs, made a significant impact on the breed. Through his progeny he produced six Show Champions, one of which became a full Champion. He worked regularly and he was field trialled. One of his most successful sons on the show ring was Sh. Ch. Russetmantle Paris, winner of eighteen CCs.

Ch. Russetmantle Troy: winner of thirteen CCs and an influential sire. Owned and bred by G. Gottlieb.

Pearce.

Ch. Russetmantle Troy – a classic point.   S. Gottlieb.

Sh. Ch. Russetmantle Paris: winner of 18 CCs. Owned and bred by G. Gottlieb.

Pearce.

Sh. Ch. Captain Quincey Of Glendun: the present breed record holder with twenty-three CCs. Owned by Jean and Paddy Winter. Bred by B. Marlow

Hartley.

Sh. Ch. Russetmantle Bee: the first Vizsla in Britain to win a Gundog Group. Owned by M. Bradbrook. Bred by G. Gottlieb.

Lindsay.

Paris was the first dog in the breed to win his first ticket at his first Championship show at six months old. His moment of glory came when he was pulled out in the last four in the Gundog Group at Crufts 1985. The present CC record holder is Sh. Ch. Captain Quincey Of Glendun, winner of twenty-three CCs, owned by Jean and Paddy Winter and bred by B. Marlow. Quincey was the first Vizsla to win Best in Show at a Championship show. He achieved this at Merseyside Gundog Championship Show in 1986 and repeated his triumph a second time at the Gundog Society of Wales Championship Show in 1987. Sadly he died in a fire in 1990. Sh. Ch. Russetmantle Bee, winner of four CCs, was the first Vizsla in Britain to win a Gundog Group. She achieved this honour at the Scottish Kennel Club Championship Show under the Canadian judge William Taylor, in 1984.

Ch. Gardenway Charlotte: winner of twenty CCs. Owned and bred by J. Perkins. Pearce.

In the late eighties two great bitches, both owned and bred by J. Perkins, dominated the show ring: Ch. Gardenway Charlotte, winner of twenty CCs, and Ch. Gardenway Dawn Run, winner of nineteen CCs. This bitch also won two Gundog Groups at Championship level: Birmingham National in 1989 and Paignton in 1989. Ch. Fandango In The Sun At Hookside has worked and trialled all his life, and has also enjoyed success in the show ring, winning seven CCs and best overall veteran at South of England Championship Show in 1991. Ch. Russetmantle Quiver, a grandson of Russetmantle Troy was a truely dual purpose Vizsla. He worked and trialled with success, and he was the winner of twenty CCs. Sadly he died of cancer at the age of six when he was at his peak in the ring – a great loss to the Russetmantle kennel. Sh. Ch. Pitswarren Levi has twelve CCs to date. This dog, owned and bred by P. Harper, won his way in the ring from a puppy and is consistently in the cards. He won Best in Show at the Hungarian Society Championship Show in 1990 and 1991. In fact, Levi and Ch. Gardenway Dawn Run were joint top Vizslas in 1991. Best of Breed at Crufts 1992 was Sally Coote's Stregaya Fleet.

Ch. Gardenway Dawn Run: winner of nineteen CCs and two Gundog Groups. Owned and bred by J. Perkins.

Sh. Ch. Fandango In The Sun At Hookside: winner of seven CCs, as well as working and trialling all his life. Owned by M. Elliote. Bred by A. Coombes.

Hartley.

Ch Russetmantle Quiver: winner of twenty CCs, he also worked and trialled with success. Owned and bred by G. Gottlieb.

Freeman.

Sh. Ch. Pitswarren Levi: winner of twelve CCs to date. Owned and bred by P. Harper.

Hartley.

Ch. Cuzco Laski: Best of Breed at Crufts 1991. This Vizsla is also worked and shot over regularly. Bred by B. Wilson. Owned by M. Pia.

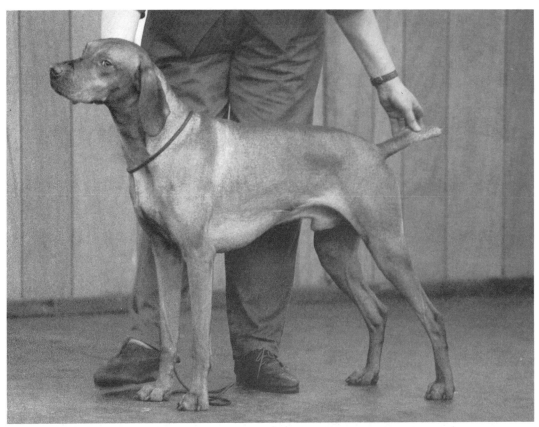

Stregaya Fleet: Best of Breed at Crufts 1992. Owned and bred by Sally Coote. Paul.

There are many Vizslas who made their mark in the breed history even though they may not have gained a title. Galfrid Gaspar was born in quarantine, his sire and dam both being Hungarian stock. His temperament was superb, he worked and trialled most of his life. He gained his junior warrant at a very early age, and although not a Champion himself, he is behind most of the successful Vizslas today. Waidman Brock is another who figures in many bloodlines; his temperament and soundness, combined with natural working ability, is firmly stamped in pedigrees of today. He sired one Show Champion and many working Vizslas, including Field Trial Champion Viszony Of Vallotta. He worked all his life. His sire was the Austrian import Bingo Vom Wurmbrandpark.

One more great bitch must be mentioned – she can never be ignored in our breed history today – Field Trial Ch. Viszony Of Vallotta, owned, bred, trained and handled by Sylvia Cox. Viszony is the only Field Trial Champion in the breed. She is by Waidman Brok ex Calversham Amber. She was shown as a youngster and later in field trial classes, but it was in the field and trialling that she came into her own. It should be appreciated that to win her title she was competing in open stakes, open to all the HPR breeds. Sylvia writes: "The August before her first birthday we had a working holiday in Scotland; it was here on the

Waidman Brok: probably did more to contribute to the success of the Vizsla in the field than any other dog in the breed. Owned and bred by L. Petrie Hay.

grouse, that we first had stars in our eyes for her. She showed terrific pace, style and stamina, but it was the 'hungry want' of every bird on the moor that showed the most. One extraordinary ability we learned in her was that she was able to adapt to whatever form of game hunting or retrieving was needed of her throughout the seasons. In the course of her life she has hunted the high tops of Scotland for Ptarmigan to everyday rabbits around the farm. She has retrieved everything from the smallest Snipe to the largest Grouse, the Capercaillie." Viszony retired with thirty-five field trial awards to her name – truly a multi-purpose Vizsla.

We must not only put emphasis on the high achievers. The backbone of the breed are all those wonderful pet companions, who fulfil the role of house dog, protector of the family, walking friend and companion – a member of the family and one who can also accompany the shooter for his pleasure. These are the unsung ambassadors of the breed.

Chapter Three

THE BREED STANDARD

The Breed Standard outlines the unique features of every breed of dog. This is the blueprint and it is the prototype that provides a fundamental reference for all who wish to advance a breed. Over many years of observing the Vizsla, it is clear that every characteristic is what it is, for a good reason. The dog's appearance and style stamp it as an individual. The Breed Standard relates to its job of work as well its conformation. At best, the working and showing Vizsla has everything to offer.

Both the British and American Breed Standards were originally based on the Hungarian Vizsla Standard, since that is the breed's country of origin. Both countries have now revised their Standards, although much of the core material taken from the Hungarian original remains relevant.

THE HUNGARIAN BREED STANDARD

CHARACTERISTICS

Medium-size, short-haired, yellow gundog of elegant appearance. It is rather lightly than heavily built, reflecting a harmony of beauty and strength. Balanced, intelligent, with vivid temperament. History writers consider the Pannion hound as one of the ancestors of the Vizsla. The yellow gundog of the Turks also played a significant role in the development of the breed. Some writers, however, date back its first appearance to

The Breed Standard relates to the Vizsla's job of work as well as to its conformation. Vizslas pictured in Hungary.

Anatomy of the Vizsla

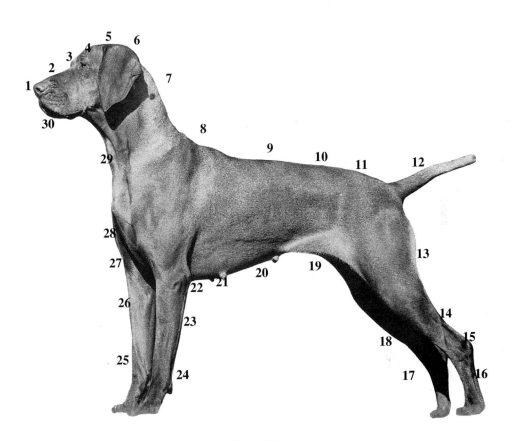

KEY

1. Nose
2. Muzzle
3. Stop
4. Forehead
5. Occiput
6. Pole joint – 2 verts
7. Neck – 7 verts
8. Withers – 8 verts
9. Back – 5 verts
10. Loin – 7 verts

11. Croup – 3 verts
12. Tail
13. Upper thigh (femur)
14. Lower thigh (tibia & fibia)
15. Hock
16. Pastern
17. Canon bone
18. Stifle
19. Tuck up
20. Belly

21. Brisket
22. Elbow
23. Forearm (radius & ulna)
24. Pastern
25. Knee
26. Forearm
27. Upper arm (humerus)
28. Chest
29. Throat
30. Lip

several years earlier. Latest researches indicate that the 'sloughi' was among the common ancestors. The first present-form specimens of the breed appeared in the early 18th century. In conformity with the modernisation of hunting habits in the 19th century, other gundogs had been used in their improvement and finally there emerged a separate yellow national dog. The breed recovered after the war to develop into its present form, characterised by the following:

It is trained easily and quickly. Its character does not tolerate rough treatment. Inherited qualities, excellent memory and good reasoning power, make it the gundog of modern times. In spite of its great passion for hunting, it likes house keeping as well. Because of this, and also because of its distinguished manner, many people keep it as a companion dog. It is widely known for its excellent ability for acclimatisation and is an untiring worker, even in immense heat. Out of its inherited traits, the following are deemed necessary: excellent scenting powers; staunch, figurative pointing; distinct trailling and retrieving qualities, love of water-work and excellent response to handling.

HEAD

Dry, noble, proportioned. The skull moderately wide, slightly domed. A slight median line, extending from the moderately developed occipital bone towards the forehead, divides the top of the head. The bridge of the nose is always straight. The foreface is well arched, neither pointed nor wide, ending in a well developed nose with nostrils well open.

Measuring the straight line linking the tip of the nose and the inner corners of the eyes, the foreface is always less than 50 per cent of the total length of the head. The fang is proportionately long, the jaw is well-developed, well-muscled. The teeth are powerful, the incisors close like scissors. The expression is vivid, intelligent, the eyes are slightly oval. The eyelids are tight. The colour of the eyes harmonise with the colour of the coat: the darker the eyes, the more desirable. The ears are of medium length, set slightly back at medium-height, and are flat against the cheek, cover the ear-holes well and end in a V-shape rounding off towards the tip.

NECK

Medium length, well-muscled, slightly arched, free from disturbing dewlaps. Set on the trunk at medium height.

TRUNK

Powerful, proportioned, slightly longer than with the quadratic breeds. The withers, pronounced, well-muscled. The back is short, straight; the line tight with the upper

Hungarian dog with undocked tail.

line, slightly rounding off towards the base of the rump. The chest is moderately wide and deep, reaching down to the elbows. The ribs are moderately arched. The shoulders are well-muscled, the shoulder blades slant, the movement is free.

LIMBS

The forelegs are straight, strong-boned, the elbows close to the body. The hind legs are well-muscled, moderately angulated; hocks slightly low set. The toes are strong, well-rounded, compact. The paws are slightly oval, the nails are strong, the pads tough.

TAIL

Slightly low set, medium thick, narrowing towards the tip. It forms aesthetic entity with the body when only three-quarters of the original length is left. Usually, one quarter is docked. If, however, the fine-lined tail is carried standardly, i.e. close to the horizontal plane, docking is not mandatory.

SKIN

The skin is tight, free from wrinkles or folds. The skin is pigmented, the nose is flesh-coloured, the lips, the eyelids and the nails are brown. The pads are slate-grey.

COAT

The hair lies flat, close to the body; it is short, and rough feeling. The belly is slightly haired. At the ears, the hair is shorter and more silky. The tail is covered with longer hair.

COLOUR

Various shades of sandy or dark sandy. Smaller white spots on the chest and on the feet are not faulted.

GAIT

Far-reaching, vigorous, smooth. While hunting, the gait is a balanced, steady canter.

HEIGHT

The ideal height for males: 56-61 cm, 22-24 inches.
For females: 52-57 cm, 20$1/2$-22$1/2$ inches.
4 cm deviation from the above is permitted in either way, if it does not disturb harmony. Static and dynamic balance, as well as symmetry, are considered much more important than proportions measured in centimetres.

TYPE FAULTS

All those structural faults or significant defects that disadvantageously influence the harmony of movement and continuous work. Major faults are: extremely light or rough structure, significant deviation from the standard, disproportioned build, short, but high structure, over-size individuals. Faults of the head are considered of major importance, such as: disproportioned, either too wide or too narrow skull and forehead; pointed, hollow, or cone-shaped head, hound head, over-expressed stop, short pointed muzzle, ram's nose. Important faults are: pendulous lips, loose skin on the head, small disproportionate, close, deep-set, or protruding light-coloured eyes; loose lids, expressionless, ill-intentioned look. Too low or too high set, narrow, twisted ears. Irregularly closing teeth, undershot or overshot by 2 mm; wry mouth, buck-tooth, scale, yellow teeth, bigger dewlaps on the neck.
Trunk: Slack muscles, loose back and narrow pelvis; short, sway-back or steep hindquarters; sagging or sunken withers; chest either not properly deep or chest too wide; flat ribs. With females, sagging belly after whelping.

*Over-expressed stop.
Paul.*

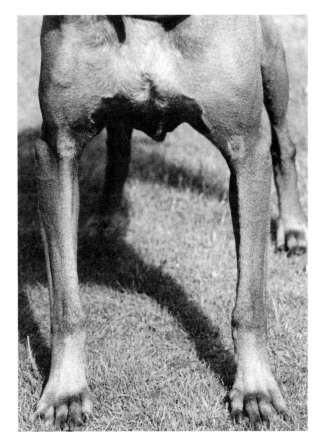

Too-wide front.

*Matthews-
Paul.*

The chest is not deep enough; it should reach to the elbow.   Paul.

Breast bone too prominent.

Paul.

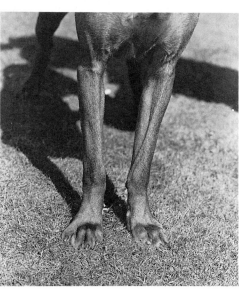

Loose feet and pasterns.

Pearce.

Limbs: Set of the legs deviating from the standard; angulations; loose, not closed, long paws.

Tail: Tail set high, carried considerably higher than the horizontal.

Coat: Thin, silky, extremely short, fine or thin, like mouse-hair; and any deviation from short hair.

Colour: Dark brown, rusty and pale yellow shades are not desirable. The darker stripe on the back (the king stripe), which is usually due to nourishment conditions, is not considered a significant fault. White spots around the throat, or marks, are faulted only if larger than 5 cm in diameter.

DISQUALIFICATION

Considerable deviations from the breed characteristics. Deviation from the standard height of more than 4 cm in either way. Parti-colour, spottiness, bigger spots on the chest, white feet. Pointed foreface, narrow greyhound-like or rough, hound-like skull. Light-coloured eyes, grey or contrasting coloured eyes. Ectrophy, entrophy, strong ram's nose; pink, slate-grey, black or spotted nose and black pigmented lips, or eyelids. Undershot; overshot more than 2 mm; wry mouth, pendulous lips, salivation, strong dewlaps. Colours lighter than wax-yellow or brown colour. Shy, weak-nerved, albino, cryptorchid or monorchid dogs. Seriously constrained faulty gait. Dysplasia of the hip-joint.

The Breed Standard of the Hungarian Vizsla in Britain was approved in 1973 by the Kennel Club; it was revised in 1975. In 1983 the Kennel Club instructed that all Breed Standards must conform in specific wording, titles and headings. Thus the British Standard was rephrased and shortened.

THE BRITISH BREED STANDARD

GENERAL APPEARANCE

Medium-sized, of distinguished appearance, robust and medium-boned.

CHARACTERISTICS

Lively, intelligent, obedient, sensitive, very affectionate and easily trained. Bred for hunting fur and feather, pointing and retrieving from land and water.

TEMPERAMENT

Lively, gentle-mannered and demonstratively affectionate, fearless and with well developed protective instinct.

HEAD AND SKULL

Head lean and noble. Skull moderately wide between ears with medium line down forehead and a moderate stop. Skull a little longer than muzzle. Muzzle, although tapering, well squared at the end. Nostrils well-developed, broad and wide. Jaws strong and powerful. Lips covering jaws completely and neither loose nor pendulous. Nose brown.

EYES

Neither deep nor prominent, of medium size, a shade darker in colour than coat. Slightly oval in shape, eyelids fitting tightly. Yellow or black eye undesirable.

EARS

Moderately low set, proportionately long with a thin skin and hanging down close to cheeks. Rounded V shape; not fleshy.

MOUTH

Sound and strong white teeth. Jaws strong with perfect, regular and complete scissor bite, i.e. upper teeth closely overlapping lower teeth and set square to the jaws. Full dentition desirable.

NECK

Strong, smooth and muscular; moderately long, arched and devoid of dewlap.

FOREQUARTERS

Shoulders well laid and muscular, elbows close to body and straight, forearm long, pasterns upright.

BODY

Back level, short, well muscled, withers high. Chest moderately broad and deep with prominent breast bone. Distance from withers to lowest part of chest equal to distance from chest to ground. Ribs well sprung and belly with a slight tuck-up beneath loin. Croup well muscled.

HINDQUARTERS

Straight when viewed from rear, thighs well developed with moderate angulation, hocks well let down.

FEET

Rounded with toes short, arched and tight. Cat-like foot is required, hare foot undesirable. Nails short, strong and a shade darker in colour than coat; dewclaws should be removed.

TAIL

Moderately thick, rather low set, customarily one-third docked. When moving carried horizontally.

GAIT/MOVEMENT

Graceful, elegant, with a lively trot and ground-covering gallop.

COAT

Short, straight, dense, smooth and shiny, feeling greasy to the touch.

COLOUR

Russet gold, small white marks on chest and feet, though acceptable, undesirable.

SIZE

Height at withers: 57-64 cms (22$1/2$-25 ins); bitches: 53-60 cms (21-23$1/2$ ins). Weight: 20-30 kgs (48$1/2$-66 lbs).

FAULTS

Any departure from these points should be considered a fault and the seriousness with which the fault should be regarded should be in exact proportion to its degree.

NOTE Male animals should have two apparently normal testicles fully descended into the scrotum.

Reproduced by kind permission of the English Kennel Club.

THE AMERICAN BREED STANDARD

GENERAL APPEARANCE

That of a medium-sized short-coated hunting dog of distinguished appearance and bearing. Robust but rather lightly built; the coat is an attractive solid golden rust. This is a dog of power and drive in the field, yet a tractable and affectionate companion in the home. It is strongly emphasized that field conditioned coats, as well as brawny or sinewy muscular condition and honorable scars indicating a working and hunting dog are never to be penalized in this dog. The qualities that make a "dual dog" are always to be appreciated not deprecated.

HEAD

Lean and muscular. Skull moderately wide between the ears with a median line down the forehead. Stop between skull and foreface is moderate, not deep. Foreface or muzzle is of equal length or slightly shorter than skull when viewed in profile, should taper gradually from stop to tip of nose. Muzzle square and deep. It must not turn up as in a "dish" face nor should it turn down. Whiskers serve a functional purpose; their removal is permitted but not preferred. Nostrils slightly open. Nose brown. Any other colour is faulty. A TOTALLY BLACK NOSE IS A DISQUALIFICATION. Ears, thin, silky and proportionately long, with rounded-leather ends, set fairly low and hanging close to cheeks. Jaws are strong with well-developed white teeth meeting in a scissor bite. Eyes medium in size and depth of setting, their surrounding tissue covering the whites. Colour of the iris should blend with the colour of the coat. Yellow or any other colour is faulty. Prominent pop-eyes are faulty. Lower eyelids should neither turn in nor out since both conditions allow seeds and dust to irritate the eye. Lips cover the jaws completely but are neither loose nor pendulous.

NECK AND BODY

Neck strong, smooth and muscular, moderately long, arched and devoid of dewlap,

"Distinguished appearance and bearing" : *Ch. Sandor Miklos Heliker.*
Owner/handler M. Heliker. Bergman.

broadening nicely into shoulders which are moderately laid back. This is mandatory to maintain balance with the moderately angulated hindquarters. Body is strong and well proportioned. Back short. Withers high and the topline slightly rounded over the loin to the set-on of the tail. Chest moderately broad and deep reaching down to the elbows. Ribs well sprung; underline exhibiting a slight tuck-up beneath the loin. Tail set just below the level of the croup, thicker at the root and docked one-third off. Ideally, it should reach to the back of the stifle joint and be carried at or near the horizontal. An undocked tail is faulty.

FOREQUARTERS

Shoulder blades proportionately long and wide, sloping moderately back and fairly close at the top. Forelegs straight and muscular with elbows close. Feet cat-like, round and compact with toes close. Nails brown and short. Pads thick and tough. Dewclaws, if any, to be removed on front and rear feet. Hare feet are faulty.

HINDQUARTERS

Hindlegs have well-developed thighs, with moderately angulated stifles and hocks in balance with the moderately laid back shoulders. They must be straight as viewed from behind. Too much angulation at the hocks is as faulty as too little. The hocks are let down and parallel to each other.

COAT

Short, smooth, dense and close-lying without wooly undercoat.

COLOR

Solid golden rust in different shadings. Solid dark mahogany red and pale yellow are faulty. Small white spots on chest are not faulted but massive areas of white on chest or white anywhere else on the body is a disqualification. Occasional white hairs on toes are acceptable but solid white extending above the toes is a disqualification. White due to ageing shall not be faulted. Any noticeable area of black in the coat is a serious fault.

GAIT

Far-reaching, light-footed, graceful and smooth. When moving at a fast trot, a properly built dog single-tracks.

SIZE

The ideal male is 22 to 24 inches at the highest point over the shoulder blades. The

ideal female is 21 to 23 inches. Because the Vizsla is meant to be a medium-sized hunter, any dog measuring more than 1½ inches over or under these limits must be disqualified.

TEMPERAMENT

A natural hunter, endowed with a good nose and above-average ability to take training. Lively, gentle-mannered, demonstrably affectionate and sensitive, though fearless with a well-developed protective instinct. Shyness, timidity or nervousness should be penalized.

DISQUALIFICATIONS

Completely black nose. Massive areas of white on chest, white anywhere else on the body, solid white extending above the toes. Any male over 25½ inches or under 20½ inches and any female over 24½ inches or under 19½ inches at the highest point over the shoulder blades.

Reproduced by kind permission of the American Kennel Club.

INTERPRETATION

The Standard is the cornerstone of the breed; we may wish it were different, we may want to change it; we may try to make the Standard fit our dogs, but, officially, we must attempt to breed Vizslas to fit the Standard. Let us therefore look at the Standard from the point of view of breeding and judging this dual-purpose hunter, pointer, retriever and discover why specific points are asked for in this context.

GENERAL APPEARANCE

The English Breed Standard is limited in its description, giving just one line, compared to the much fuller descriptions in both the Hungarian and American Standards. The American Standard pays tribute to the working side of the breed, stating that it is strongly emphasized that field scars indicate working and hunting dogs, and such a Vizsla must not be penalized. The qualities that make a 'dual dog' are always to be appreciated not deprecated."

This important statement can only contribute to the advancement of the breed. I hope that 'honorable scars' would be accepted by British judges, although I am not entirely confident. I was advised years ago, to wrap my winning dog up in cotton wool, and to leave a working dog at home. We should all be proud to show our gundogs, scars and all.

The dual purpose hunter, pointer retriever: Futaki Lenke.
Owned and bred by Chauncey Smith, United States.

"Medium-sized, of distinguished appearance, robust and medium-boned." Galfrid Odo and Sh. Ch. Galfrid Mia: owned and bred by A. Boys, Britain.
Pearce.

*Temperament is all:
Galfrid Gasper and
Sh. Ch. Galfrid Jade.
Owned and bred by
A. Boys.*

                                        Pearce.

A shy, fine boned narcissistic, weedy individual, with general lack of substance, will not do in the field. The wording 'lightly boned' has been changed in the English Standard to 'medium boned', giving more guidance for a medium-sized dog; whereas the American Standard still asks for a lightly built dog.

CHARACTERISTICS

If the owner has experience, the Vizsla can be house trained in a matter of days, and trained in basic obedience. But mistimed firmness or too much pressure, too early, can make the dog obstinate and over-dependent. Training it to work calls for patience and dedication. Professional trainers or ambitious handlers can find this breed exasperating; it has to be given time. The HPRs have a complicated pattern of working which means the dog cannot reach its full potential unless it shows instinct and willingness to learn.

TEMPERAMENT

Temperament is all; a good-looking animal, however beautiful, is not worth owning if it does not relate to humans.

Ch. Russetmantle Troy showing an aristocratic head.   *Marc Henrie.*

HEAD AND SKULL

The word 'gaunt' has been deleted from the English Standard and 'lean' has replaced it. 'Gaunt' in the Oxford Dictionary is defined as "famished, slim and haggard", which seemed rather harsh. The muzzle measurement has been corrected. The original translation was faulty, asking for the muzzle to be longer than the skull. Thankfully, no breeder attempted to breed this fault in, although it confused one or two judges! A snipey muzzle is not acceptable, for the dog will not be able to hold or carry game on land.

EYES

The eyes are usually the first feature the attention settles on when assessing a dog. The Vizsla's eye expresses its nature; it is not the distant gaze-hound look, but a warm, soft, gentle, bold one. Its demeanour should be extrovert. The whole character of the dog is in its alertness and its interest in what is going on around it. If a dog shows a withdrawn, guarded expression, it is not likely to want to please its people or its shooting companion.

Condor v Windesheram: The Vizsla will carry the heaviest game if it has the will.

EARS

What a wealth of feeling the ears express! When the Vizsla is standing alert with ears forward, it truly has a noble and fearless aspect. The ear must reach the corner of the mouth or the head lacks proportion.

MOUTH

It is essential that the Vizsla has a strong jaw, but it must not be hard-mouthed; it has to retrieve game gently to hand, with no sign of damage, however heavy. A good, big drake could weigh three to four kilos, and a blue mountain hare might weigh four to five kilos or more.

NECK

It is sad that the English Breed Standard is so restrained in wording. The American equivalent: "The neck broadens nicely into the shoulders, which are moderately laid back", gives much more of an image to work on .

The neck is the base to which are anchored the principal muscles that hold in position, and operate, the movement of bones of the dog's forehand. This breed will carry the heaviest game if it has the will. A Canada Goose was shot out on the marshlands one season, and it was retrieved by a Vizsla, who carried it a fair distance. The weight of the bird must have been approximately fourteen kilos. Even so, the dog managed the task, with its head held high, demonstrating the importance of a strong muscular neck.

Ch. Russetmantle Quiver: The Vizsla is not square but slightly longer in the body than in height. The dog should not look like a Pointer; the difference should be maintained.

FOREQUARTERS

I think it is generally agreed among knowledgeable breeders that the construction of the Vizsla's forequarters has been a problem to correct, but now 'fronts' have greatly improved. It is essential that the angulation in the conformation throughout is correct. Great stress is put on all the joints in a lively dog, especially in a working gundog. The whole construction and balance can be put out if there are fundamental faults. A straight shoulder, loose elbows, slack pasterns and flat feet, will tire a dog. The term 'upright pasterns', used in the English Breed Standard, needs to be qualified. The joint is a shock absorber, and thus has to have some 'spring' or 'give'.

BODY

The Hungarian Breed Standard states that the trunk is slightly longer than with the quadratic breeds (square). This is an omission in the English and American Standards. Nor is the upper arm (humerus) mentioned. The shoulder blade and the upper arm should be of equal length, giving the angulation of the shoulders. This is the measurement in most gundog breeds.

This omission could lead to a fundamental change in the anatomy of the Vizsla. At the Official International Conference of The Breeders of Hungarian Breeds in 1982, Miklos Farkashazi went over the Vizsla Standard, and he stated: "The Vizsla is not square but slightly longer in the body than in height. The dog should not look like a pointer, nor should he become as strong and as fast a dog as the English Pointer; the difference should be maintained."

The English Standard states: "The distance from the withers to the lower part of the chest is equal to the distance from the chest to the ground" and this is not described so specifically in the American Standard. A working dog needs plenty of 'heart room', to expand its lungs as well. A slabsided, narrow-chested animal, with no depth, would be a short stayer in the field, and it would be prevented from pushing itself to the limit of its endurance.

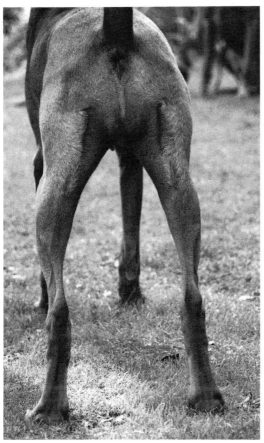

Hindquarters: "straight when viewed from rear".   *Paul.*

HINDQUARTERS

The English Standard uses the words 'muscular' and 'moderate' throughout, for good reason. The Vizsla must be fit; in a working day it may be on heavy plough, sweeping stubble fields, high roots, working up hedges and thick cover. Its quarters need to be strong and powerful with plenty of drive. If it were over-angulated it would have speed like a Greyhound, but only for short distances. The Vizsla needs to be a stayer. The English Standard leaves out the angulation of the stifle altogether and confines itself to the hocks being "well let down". The American Standard asks for moderately angulated stifles and hocks in balance with the moderately laid back shoulder.

FEET

The hare foot is for high speed, the cat foot is shorter and more compact, reducing leverage action, and lessening the strain on the ligaments. Road work can help to muscle up a young animal's foot, but a poorly constructed foot will never tighten.

TAIL

The Vizsla uses its tail expressively, and never more than when it sees its master. This is a breed that communicates every nuance of feeling with its eyes, ears and tail. Docking is a very controversial subject; the Vizsla's long, thin, slashing tail can get torn and damaged in thick cover, putting the dog out for the season's work. Once injured, a tail takes a long time to heal. Discomfort caused when docking at three days old seems nothing to the pain that could be incurred when the dog is older.

A gay tail is a bad fault. The English Standard asks for a horizontal tail carriage at all times, and in the ring the handler holds the tail level. The American Vizsla, in the ring, is often handled with the tail held above the level of the back, and in the field the Vizsla is expected to hold its tail stiff and upright when it is on point. The reason for this is that the tail indicates the dog's position in dense cover. .

GAIT/MOVEMENT

What can be more thrilling than the Vizsla quartering out at a distance from its handler, but in control, galloping at a steady rhythmical pace, using its game-finding instinct? This is a most graceful, elegant dog when its trot is lively, daisy-clipping as it goes. How it feels and how it looks, interact. If it does not have a positive mental and physical attitude, it can be inhibited in every way by its lack of initiative, drive and character.

The English Standard asks for a lively trot. The American Standard states: "When moving at a fast trot, a properly built dog single-tracks." In normal canine movement the 'single-tracking' tendency is for the legs to incline more and more under the body, as the speed increases, and eventually the paws come to travel in a single line. This term is rarely used in the UK; in the ring, dogs do not trot at a great speed. I am told that, generally speaking, the movement of the best Vizslas in the USA far surpasses anything in the UK. Such emphasis is placed on the extension, front and rear when trotting, that the dog is carried along at a tremendous pace.

In the field the American dogs are fast, hard-going, bold and birdy. In Britain systematic controlled ground coverage is required, with the emphasis always on steadiness.

COAT

The Vizsla's coat must be one of the easiest to manage. If a dog is healthy and fit, it hardly needs any care. A rubber glove is all that is required to remove mud or moulting hair. The slight greasiness is necessary as protection. Although sparse beneath its belly, a hard-going dog takes little notice. It loves nothing more than being stroked, and its coat is a delight to touch.

Gait: "graceful and elegant." Aust. Ch. Russetmantle Goosander. Owned by Fay Harris, bred by Gay Gottlieb. *R. Twigg.*

COLOUR

Russet gold is now the only term accepted by the English Kennel Club. Formerly, when puppies were registered, the terms red, silver beige, red golden and white, sandy yellow and brown-and-tan were being used under "colour". In general, there is less variation in colour than in the seventies and eighties. Some puppies in a litter may appear to have too much white on the chest and feet, but invariably it disappears after several days. An ageing Vizsla can go white early on. In the American Standard "massive white" was introduced under 'Disqualifications' in 1982. Somewhere along the line dogs had started to appear at Field trials with an excess amount of white. It is thought that the Vizsla was being out-crossed to the Pointer to improve performance in the field. As a consequence the Magyar Vizsla Society was formed in an effort to deal with the situation. It has become confusing now for judges to know exactly when to disqualify, although as in the English Standard, a small amount of white (5cms) is permissible, and a small amount of white spots on the chest (USA) is not faulted. But white shoulders, white under the neck, under the brisket, solid white coming way up over the toes and legs, is not allowed. My comment, as a judge, is that in Britain we rarely see white beyond that which is acceptable, and I have withheld a first because a Vizsla under me had a little more. We know that in Hungary, many years ago, too much white was a problem, so we know the gene for white is well and truly present.

The English Standard does not describe the uniqueness of the Vizsla's colour: its nose, eye lids, nails, pads and its skin are neither pink nor black, but blend in with its coat colour.

The American Standard states solid golden rust in different shadings, which gives the breeder a wide choice. However, russet gold in the English Standard does not mean that there is not a variation; describing the 'senses' is infinitely complex. The Golden Pointer is a glorious colour: when the sun is on its back or it is running in autumn leaves or on a fresh spring grass, it must be the most stunning of all the HPRs.

SIZE

The Breed Standard emphasises 'moderate' throughout, and that is how the Vizsla should be overall, which is not easy for the breeder to achieve. If your Vizsla is too large or too small it will make no difference to its excellence as a companion, but it will affect a breeding programme. The American Standard is specific in demanding: "Any dog measuring more than one and a half inches over or under the limits must be disqualified." The British limit is one inch higher than the American dogs, and there is no disqualification for anything taller. It is up to the judge in the ring to penalise or not.

Chapter Four

THE WIRE-HAIRED VIZSLA

The wire-haired Vizsla is recognised as pure-bred in many countries today. On the continent they are very highly thought of. Although they are recognised by the Canadian Kennel Club, in America the AKC does not recognise them, and the Vizsla Club of America does not class them as a sub-type, so the wire-haired Vizsla, known as 'Uplanders' in the USA, cannot gain official recognition. But in France, for instance, there are wire-haired Vizslas that have qualified well in the field and in the show ring at Championship level, as there are in Hungary, Holland, Austria, Germany and Switzerland.

Working Vizslas in Hungary have many demands made on them; water-work and wild fowling on the great lakes is popular and profitable, since many sportsmen travel to Hungary to shoot. Therefore a dog who can work in these conditions is essential, and the wire-haired Vizsla, which can shed water easily from its thicker, warmer coat has an advantage over the short-haired type. When I judged wire-haired Vizslas in Switzerland I found the coat type very varied, but the dog I gave the CAC and Best of Breed to was very handsome; his overall conformation was excellent. He had a proud demeanour and great presence. I learned later that he worked for the Red Cross in searching and rescuing in the mountains – a true multi-purpose dog.

In Britain two wire-hairs were imported in the late seventies by Douglas Appleton. The first to arrive was Aranyos Tizsla Dudas – pet name 'Zloty'. She was later owned and handled by David Mic Layton of the Midlander prefix. Zloty was shown with some success

'Zloty' and 'Boros: the first two wire-hairs in Britain.   *Fisher.*

in 'Any Variety Not Separately Classified'. A mate arrived in 1983, Boros Tyankp Gulyas Of Carril Temple, but unfortunately Zloty never came into whelp. In 1990 Sheila Gray (Abbeystag) and Anna Coombes (Castlefield) imported two wire-haired puppies, a dog and a bitch, from Hungary. The dog, Amor, is bred by Istvanne Nebehaj, and the bitch, Abafia Maya, is bred by Istvan Farkashazi. Both dogs have come out of their quarantine period well. They have excellent temperaments, and they endear themselves wherever they go.

The Hungarian Breed Standard for the wire-haired is virtually the same as the Standard for the short-haired, except for the coat and the stipulation for stronger bones. The difference in coat is given in detail, and it is essential to note that, although the beard stands up and away, as do the eyebrows, the coat lies flat and close. Its jacket is rather similar to the Irish Terrier; it must not be wavy or woolly, nor wild or profuse. The coat usually falls out in the Spring, but in general, it needs little grooming and no trimming. It does not matt after getting wet. Sheila Gray states: "For myself, the greatest joy in living with the wire-haired Vizsla is the cheeky expression on their whiskery faces!"

Abafia Hires Humor, Amor's sire at a Hungarian show.

Sh. Ch. 'Volpi'. Owned and bred by Madame Parent in France.

Madame Parent has bred short-hairs and wire-hairs in France for many years, and she is "passionate" about the wire-haired variety. She finds them very intelligent, gentle, and happy to work and learn. She finds them calmer than the smooth-coated Vizsla, and "more of a clown, if that is possible!" She has trained and worked her wire-hairs, the most successful being 'Volpi', a Show Champion in France, Holland, Luxembourg, a European and International Show Champion, with qualifications in the field in France, Belgium, and Hungary. His sire is a World Show Champion.

Madame Parent states: "Puppies are born with smooth coats. Then, from about six weeks to four months the difference can be seen between the different qualities of fur. Approximately ten to twenty percent of puppies will stay smooth (but they cannot be registered as smooth because the breeds are separate now, not a breed with two varieties) and approximately ten to twenty per cent will have long, curly or woolly coats. Thus in a litter of ten puppies, one or two would be smooth, and of the wire-hairs, one or two would have an incorrect coat."

THE HUNGARIAN BREED STANDARD

Medium-size, strong-built, yellow, wire-haired gundog, with bones stronger than that of the short-haired variety. Because it is slightly stronger than the short-haired and, especially because its coat texture is resistant to cold and water, it is a favourable variety for water work and work on difficult terrain and marshland. In spite of its more robust appearance, it bears resemblance to the elegance of the short-haired Hungarian Vizsla. It is intelligent, affectionate, balanced.

It dates back to the 30s of the 20th century. The German Wire-haired Pointer played a part in its development. Besides fixing new features, the selective breeding throughout the decades laid a great stress upon the working abilities, since the aim of the breeding work was to develop a multi-purpose, hard working Vizsla breed. With this breeding aim accomplished, a concern shared by the breed enthusiasts today is to achieve a further homogeneity in form and especially in the texture of the coat. Considering the qualities, it is in the character that it best resembles the short-haired Vizsla. It is easy to handle, learns quickly and is sensitive to rough treatment. It has good scenting power, especially likes water-work and likes retrieving work. In style, vigour and pointing, it equals any of the short-haired Pointers of the continent.

HEAD

Proportioned; the skull is moderately wide, slightly domed, the foreface is somewhat shorter than the skull, the stop is moderate, the arches of the eyes are strong. With its characteristic coating the head is marked, slightly square. The bridge of the nose is straight, and ends wide. The jaw is developed, well-muscled, the teeth are powerful, the incisors close like scissors. The lips are moderately tight, but not pendulous. The

Cardoff Du Dumaine St Hubert: Best of Breed French National 1991. Owned by Madame Richards. Bred by Madame Parent.

expression is vivid, intelligent; the eyelids are tight, the eyes slightly oval.

The eyes are harmonized with the colour of the coat, but darker eye colour is desirable. The ears are set at medium height, are of medium length and cover the ear holes well.

NECK

Medium-length, well-muscled, slightly arched, free from disturbing dewlaps.

TRUNK

Robust and well-proportioned, longer than with the quadratic breeds; the withers well-muscled. The back is short and straight; the loin taut; the upper line slightly rounding off towards the rump base. The chest is powerfully developed, deep, reaching down at least to the elbows. The ribs are moderately arched, the shoulders are well-muscled, the shoulder blades are properly slanted, allowing free movement.

LIMBS

The forelegs are straight, strong-boned, with elbows close to the body; slightly let-down hocks; toes are strong, well-arched, close; the paws are slightly oval-shaped. The nails are strong, the pads hard.

TAIL

Set slightly low, medium thick, narrowing towards the tip. One-third is docked.

SKIN

Pigmented, taut, without wrinkles or holds. The nose is flesh-coloured; the lips, the edge of the eyelids and the nails are brown. The pads are slate-grey.

COAT

Short and rough at the foreface, with small beard at the chin. Short and rough on the top of the head. The hair of the ears is nearly the same as that of the short-haired Hungarian Vizsla. The hair at the eyebrows is dense and hard. On the neck and the trunk, there is 2–4 cm long, wiry, hard outer-coat, lying close to the body, with under-coat. The coat is shorter at the lower end of the limbs, on the lower part of the chest and on the belly. At the back edges of the limbs, longer hair is permissible. The structure of the entire coat must serve the defence of the body against adverse weather conditions and injuries. On the paws and between the toes, the hair is shorter and softer. The tail is covered with dense, thick coat. The colour of the coat is different shades of sandy yellow. Smaller white spots on the chest and at the feet are not faulted.

GAIT

Vigorous, harmonious, far-reaching. During work, hunting, the characteristic gait is medium-pace canter.

HEIGHT

The ideal height is:
males 58–62cm
females 54–58cm.

Deviation of 3cm either way is permissible if, otherwise, the dog remains harmonious. Static and dynamic balance as well as symmetry are much more important than proportions measured in centimetres.

FAULTS

Faults of the head are considered of major importance, such as: disproportioned, either too wide or too narrow skull and forehead, pointed, hollow or cone-shaped head; hound-head, too strong stop; short, pointed foreface or ram's nose.

Major faults are: pendulous lips, loose skin on the head; small, disproportioned, close, deep-set or protruding light eyes; pendulous eyelids; expressionless, ill-tempered look. Too low or too high set, narrow, twisted ears. Irregularly closing teeth; undershot; overshot over 2mm, wry mouth, buck-tooth, scale; yellow teeth; bigger dewlap on the neck.

Trunk: Slack muscles; loose back and narrow pelvis; short sway-back or steep hindquarters; sagging or sunken withers; chest either not properly deep or too wide; flat ribs. With females, sagging belly following whelping.

Limbs: Set of the legs deviating from the Standard, bad angulations; loose, not closed, long paws.

Tail: Not properly docked or curled.

Coat: Soft, thin, long, wavy hair. Lack of undercoat. Too short, and thin hair on the head, limbs or sides, or on the lower part of belly and chest. Curly or griffon hair or woolly, soft hair on the head are faulted. Major fault: hair parting along the line of the backbone.

Colour: Dark brown, rusty or pale yellow shades are undesirable. A darker stripe on the back (the king stripe), which is usually due to nourishment conditions, is not considered a major fault. White spot or marks around the throat are faulted only if larger in diameter than 5cm.

Disqualifications

Considerable deviations from the breed characteristics. Deviation in height of more than 3cm in either way. Parti-colour, spottiness, bigger white spots on the chest, white feet. Pointed foreface, narrow, Greyhound-like or rough, hound-like skull. Very light eyes, grey or contrasting coloured eyes; ectropy, entropy. Strong ram's nose, pink, slate-grey, black or spotted nose; black pigmented lips or eyelids. Undershot; overshot more than 2mm, wry-mouth, pendulous lips, salivation, strong dewlaps. Brown colour or colours lighter than whey-yellow. Shy, weak-nerved, albino, cryptorchid or monorchid dogs. Seriously constrained, faulty gait. Dysplasia of the hip-joint.

THE LONG-HAIRED VIZSLA

The long-haired Vizsla is not recognised as a separate breed in Hungary, nor in any other country. There is no Breed Standard, although the Weimaraner and the German Short-haired Pointer both have such mutations and these are accepted as pure-bred and registered as such. In Britain they appear in litters from time to time, and although they cannot be shown or

Waidman Yogo Bear: a long-haired Vizsla. Owned and bred by L. Petrie Hay.

field-trialled, this delightfully attractive Vizsla gathers admirers wherever it is seen.

It is reported that in 1937 an Irish Setter was mated to a short-haired Vizsla, Kobra Z Povazio, which would appear to be the origin of long-hairs today. Louise Petrie Hay (Waidman), one of the pioneers of the breed, deduces that long hair, when present, is a dominant gene; thus the throwback can be produced from mating two short-hairs. This is apparently not unusual when there is a coat complex. On the occasions of British stock being put to imports from three different countries, Hungary, Holland and the USA, long-hairs have appeared.

These fascinating Vizslas have varying coats – some have more feathering than others; but apart from the coat, there is no more deviation from the Breed Standard than there is with short-hairs. The long-hairs are highly regarded in the field; their performance is excellent, and as such, they are in demand. They tend to have the setting stance of the Setter, rather than the higher stance of the Pointer. It takes a few days to recognise a long-haired whelp: the difference becomes apparent as the coat grows wavy on the ears and long hair appears between the toes. I have seen long-hairs in Holland and Switzerland, and they all seem to have in common a gentle aspect, which makes them lovable companions.

Chapter Five

THE SHOW RING

The most prestigious of all-breed dog shows in America must be 'Westminster' in New York City. All the dog world flocks to see this spectacular show. But for the Vizsla in America, the Nationals must be the greatest occasion; the National Vizsla Show Specialties are where the breed has four or five days of field, show, obedience, sweepstake and junior showmanship events. To see such a gathering of Vizslas must be very exciting indeed. The British show season starts off with Crufts, known as the 'greatest show in the world'. Entry for competition is restricted to dogs who have qualified at other Championship shows during the preceding year. It is a marvellous spectacle, and one which attracts breeders and enthusiasts from all over the world. The Hungarian Vizsla entries are in the hundreds these days.

Comparing the British and American systems of showing in all their aspects, there seems to be quite a difference. Many Vizslas are professionally handled to "finish" in the USA – the British term is "made up", both meaning that the dog has achieved Champion status. In Britain the Hungarian Vizsla has to qualify in the field as well, to gain the full title of Champion. The American professional handler charges a fixed fee, and additional charges are incurred as the dog proceeds from the Breed to Group, to Best in Show. The handler is also entitled to all the prize money. The dog will usually remain with its handler for all or part of its show career. The advantage is that the professional will win more often: a dog fares better in a Group and for Best in Show when it is shown to best advantage.

In the main, the British showing scene is on a much lower key, compared with the style and razzmatazz, and sheer showmanship of the American scene, although obviously this does not affect the quality of the dogs. Type tends to differ from state to state, but this also

A Championship Show: Progression from puppy classes to Best in Show

IN BRITAIN

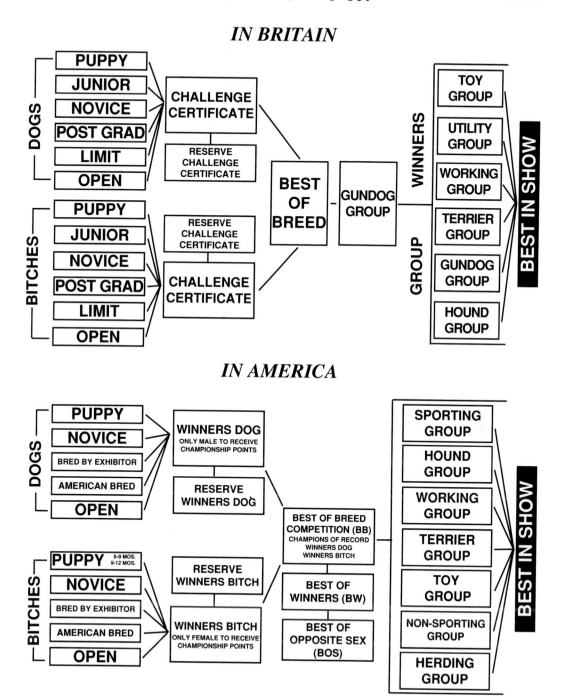

IN AMERICA

occurs in Britain, between the different prefixes. Chauncey Smith comments: "I would say there is a difference in type not necessarily from state to state, but from East to Mid-West to West. More of East Coast dogs are bred from show stock, there are few breeders using hunting stock, and the same situation is probably true on the West Coast. In the Mid-West more of the people still hunt their dogs than in any other part of the United States. There is definitely a difference in appearance."

The Vizslas in Britain are shown by the breeder/owner, and the handling can range from excellent to poor. Every professional was an amateur at one time, and all the great breeders, handlers, and judges came into the fancy as amateurs, and they learnt their particular craft with dedication. Showing can be treated as a hobby, a chance to meet friends and a social occasion, or, for the more ambitious, it is an event where the dedicated breeder and owner, wishing to produce stock of excellence, has a chance to assess and be assessed against the Breed Standard and the breed. The gathering together of breed enthusiasts is also a way of monitoring a breed. It is also an opportunity for the breed to be seen, and for newcomers to be introduced to more Vizslas than they are ever likely to see anywhere else; and of course, the purpose of showing can be one of the ways to perpetuate the Vizsla's unique qualities.

HANDLING

The art of handling is to have belief and confidence in yourself, and your dog, showing it to the best advantage with knowledge and skill. How the handler feels and performs reflects on any dog. The Vizsla, in particular, relates very closely with its handler, reflecting our moods, our sadnesses and depressions, happiness and joyfulness. Sometimes that extra something, called style, that we see in the ring, is the tension and excitement of the occasion affecting the handler's and the Vizsla's performance. The word 'showmanship' is apt – they both present the picture: "Here we are, look at us!" It is an enthralling moment for judge and spectators. It is understood that every dog has its faults; good handling consists of highlighting its virtues, poor handling accentuates the dog's weaknesses. So how do you begin to learn to handle your Vizsla in the show ring? First, get to know your Vizsla; there is no reason why the exhibitor needs to feel that the judge is uniquely capable of assessing a dog. The owner can learn to do this for himself. I am convinced that most handlers know their own dog's faults; they may own up to them to themselves, but they have difficulty in accepting them. Examine and study the points of your Vizsla with the Breed Standard. There, before you, are all the hallmarks of the breed. Compare and contrast every characteristic. For instance, how do you interpret a 'moderate stop'? Go over your Vizsla, and many more, if you can. Once you have compared your Vizsla with the blueprint, you will start to get your eye in.

YOUR PUPPY

The Vizsla puppy can start to learn to stand and trot very early on; it is all part of its

Russetmantle Cloud at eight weeks: Firmness, patience and determination will assure the puppy that you mean to succeed. (The ears are too long).   S. Gottlieb.

conditioning. Showing is an extension of its willingness to please you. We all know this breed's stubborn streak and its clowning antics, but firmness and patience, and a determination on your part, will assure the dog that you mean to succeed. Give a lot of leeway to a puppy; its concentration is not too good for any length of time, but a high degree of showing ability can be perfected as it matures.

Always use the same lead for practising. The dog will soon learn that this means a learning time. You will need to be guided by individual temperament when standing a dog. If it is placid, it may behave better than a livewire, but both types can become bored just as quickly. The lively one may turn out better in the long run. That energy can be an asset in the ring; nothing is worse than a plodder, either in the ring or in the field. All puppies should enjoy these sessions, and you should praise with your hands and your voice. Using force or man-handling and mauling, will result in the dog hating the whole idea, and it will feel the show ring means punishment, tension and anger. It will become one of those unhappy Vizslas in the ring who tuck up and clamp their tails between their legs, hoping it will all be over soon.

LEARNING TO STAND YOUR PUPPY

Kneel down with the puppy in front of you, with your right hand on its chest or neck, gently stroking, but holding it if it moves. Run your left hand over and over its back, talking to it soothingly. Then you can either place each back leg separately, or put your hand between its hind legs, and lightly lift them and place them so that the puppy stands balanced. The idea is for the puppy to feel comfortable, so it will learn to like that feeling. Hold the tail horizontal,

Standing your puppy: kneel down and put your right hand on the puppy's chest, and place each back leg separately. Handled by M. Williams.

Pearce.

The idea is for the puppy to feel comfortable. Handled by M. Williams.

Pearce.

on the flat of your hand, and make sure the puppy knows what you want it to do, by saying "Stand". It does not matter, at first, how it stands, or how long it stands for; it should be just enough for it to get the message, and to know it has done as you asked. Make a great fuss of the puppy, and end on a good note. Every time do a little bit more, but never over-do it.

LEARNING TO TROT YOUR PUPPY

Most puppies like trotting on the lead; encourage the pup to run by your side, and if it jumps up, push it down saying "No", and then "Trot on", so that it knows that this is not playtime. Once the puppy is going forward, talk to it all the time; this will help to keep its attention, and it will be eager to listen. Later on, you can teach your puppy to trot in a triangle, but there is no hurry. Meanwhile, the pup needs to socialise: a show can be a frightening experience for a six-month-old puppy unless it is used to other dogs, loud noises and crowds of people. You should also allow other people to feel the puppy all over, as a judge would, and to examine its teeth. Many owners take their puppies to ring craft (handling) classes: mixing with dogs and people at a busy site such as this, is ideal.

CHOOSE YOUR METHOD

Sooner or later you will have to decide what method of handling you wish to adopt. Taking the Breed Standard as the guideline, the Vizsla should look lively and intelligent, have an excellent nose, be obedient, sensitive and easily trained. It must have a distinguished appearance. How can you get your dog to display these qualities? Stringing your Vizsla up is not going to help it look distinguished, nor is propping it up, so that its head is held up in the air and its back is hunched. The skill is to allow your dog to look as if it is standing free and alert, bold and interested with an outward aspect, demonstrating the independent temperament it needs to have. However, this is by no means easy to achieve. It helps if you have an image in your mind of how you would like to see your dog, and this is a goal to work towards.

   All handlers devise their own technique, but here is the basic method that can be adapted. Stand your Vizsla in front of you, place the front legs perpendicular to the floor, taking the line from the wither. Then hold the lead up behind the dog's ears with the right hand, and run the left hand down its back, placing the back legs, each in turn, so that the dog is balanced and covers the ground well. There should be plenty of space between the front and back legs, and the dog must take its weight equally on all four feet.

Connie Johnson's American Sageacre Vizslas: The skill is to allow your dog to look free and alert, bold and interested, with an outward aspect demonstrating its independent character.   *J. McMillan.*

SETTING YOUR DOG UP

Russetmantle Noel at nine months. Place the front legs perpendicular to the floor, taking the line from the wither. Handler G. Gottlieb.

S. Hart.

Hold the lead up behind the dog's ears with the right hand.

S. Hart.

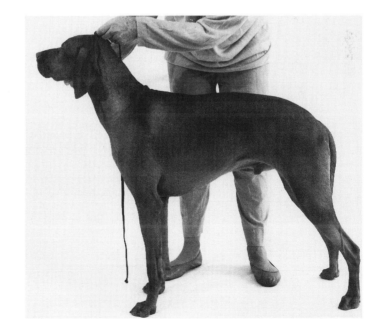

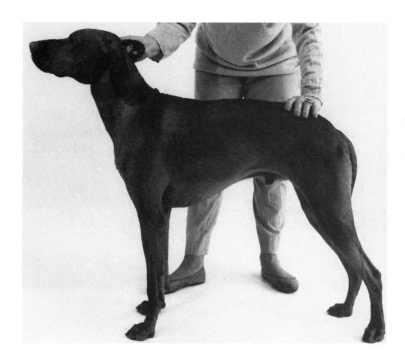

*Run the left
hand down the
dog's back.*

S. Hart.

*Place the back
legs, each in
turn.*

S. Hart.

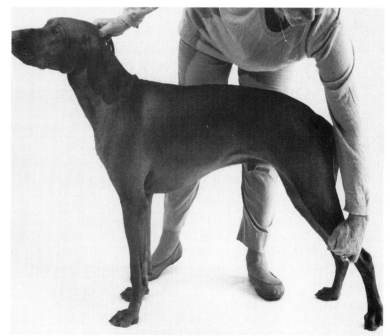

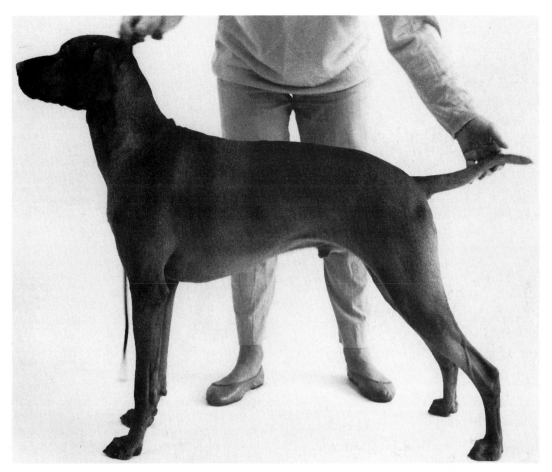

The dog will only be comfortable when it is correctly balanced. S. *Hart.*

Check the front again, and either hold the lead up behind its ears – not too tightly – or if you prefer, steady the dog's head with your right hand, holding the muzzle lightly in the ridge of its jawbones. Most Vizslas dislike having their heads held, so ideally you will come to the mutual agreement that you won't hold your dog's head, as long as it holds it up, and looks straight ahead! Finally, hold the tail horizontally in your outstretched hand.

When you are practising, try standing with your Vizsla in front of a mirror; it is surprising what dreadful mistakes we can make without being aware of them. This includes overstretching – and what we may think is an elegant sweep of the back legs, is, in reality, forcing the stifles to appear straight. Likewise, the front legs can be stretched too far forward, so the dog looks as if it is going to do the splits. Often a dog will misbehave, because it is set up badly, and its frame is distorted into a stance that is physically impossible for it to bear. A dog will only feel comfortable when it is correctly balanced.

FAULTS

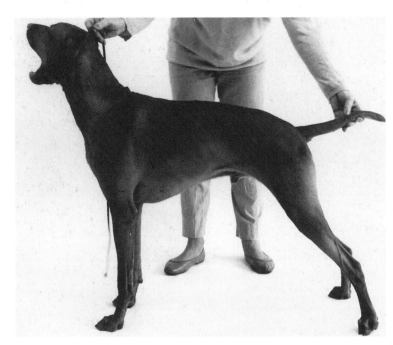

*'Over-stretching'
looks bad, and is
uncomfortable for
the dog.*

S. Hart.

*The dog must have
plenty of space
between front and
back legs. This dog
does not 'cover the
ground.'*

S. Hart.

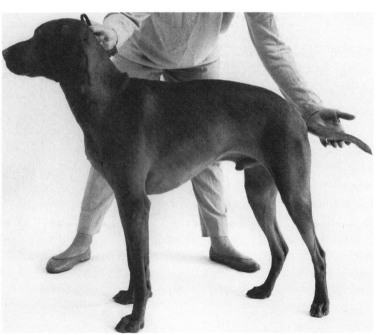

This dog is 'off balance'. Its legs are too far forward and its head is held too high.
Sh. Ch. Russetmantle Paris. Handler to demonstrate: M. Williams. *Pearce.*

Your attitude is all-important; if you set your dog up feeling apologetic, or thinking that it is going to misbehave, and vainly hoping that it will look OK when the judge comes round, then the dog will sense your feelings and react accordingly. However, if the dog is is set up firmly, with a no-nonsense, positive approach, it will know you mean business.

GAITING

The trot demonstrates the dog's structure functioning at its most effective. If a youngster has natural balance, i.e. symmetry, with no part too big or too small in relation to another part, you will find that it usually prefers to trot rather than walk, as this is a comfortable pace for it. I am always pleased to see a puppy start to trot out; it gives me an indication that everything is in the right place.

When the judge wants to assess your Vizsla's movement you will be asked to trot it in a triangle and straight up and down. Remember to never allow yourself to come between the judge and your dog. When practising, always keep the dog on your left side, and use its natural speed and ability, to move in complete harmony. We should remind ourselves that our dogs are perfectly capable of free and efficient movement on their own. The lead should be neither too tight nor too loose, and the head must stay at the same height throughout; at the same time, the dog must be collected. If a dog slops along, or charges ahead, the judge cannot see whether it moves correctly.

If you can find someone to play judge, whose comment and advice you respect, it will be time well spent. Handlers need to be aware of particular problems. A large person needs to be aware that body language can be very threatening, and a small, frail person is going to have difficulties with a big, bouncing youngster. The voice is another important factor. Talk to your dog, make it aware of your authority and what you require. If the dog is worried, it needs reassurance. A deep, gruff voice like a growl is fine for disciplining, but not for praise, so the tone needs to change. Have you noticed that if you use a little baby voice, a dog will wag its tail?

When you are in the ring, always keep your eye on the judge; your dog should look good at all times. Keep showing your dog, even after the judge has made unofficial placings. Give yourself space and time; you have come a long way and spent money, and it is your right to feel you have been given enough attention from the judge. Allow yourself an extra second or two when you set your dog up, so you can make sure it looks its best for the judge's inspection. Finally, if you feel bored, your dog will also be bored. Give it an exciting time, and it will respond. However, if your Vizsla will not show for you, look to see if there is something that you are not dealing with correctly. If a dog is not working for you, never blame the dog; blame the handler. The excuse that "My dog does not like the show ring", or "My dog won't behave in the ring", says more about the owner than the dog.

SPORTSMANSHIP IN THE RING

Never show poor sportsmanship, however bad you feel. Win graciously, and lose graciously. Ultimately, we should all be concerned with the quality and welfare of our Vizslas. Whether we agree with the results or not, our behaviour in the ring should be without fault. There is nothing so undignified as a poor loser, who cannot contain his feelings. We can learn much from the professional handler in this respect.

WHAT THE JUDGES LOOK FOR

It is the judge's prerogative to decide, in his opinion, which dogs best display the characteristics of the Breed Standard. He wants to see the dog standing and moving so that he can assess breed type, balance, conformation, soundness and temperament. Some judges will put more emphasis on movement, some on breed type, some will go over a dog minutely, others hardly handle at all. But the judge's decision is final.

Chapter Six

THE PRINCIPLES
OF BREEDING

The principles of breeding seem simple enough. Breeding like with like, begets like. Selection is the keystone to dog breeding. In order to maintain the highest quality breeding stock, only the best of the offspring are bred from, and the purpose in selecting brood stock is to increase the deposit of desirable genes. The scientist, Mendel, produced the accepted theory, that the offspring of any mating can only carry in equal parts the genes or characteristics of the parents, and only a quarter each of the grandparents. The more closely bred the parents, the more the characteristics would be undiluted and strengthened. Further related matings from the offspring would intensify the characteristics. This brings us to the question: Why can't we inter-breed repeatedly from the purest stock available – mother to son, father to daughter, brother to sister? The answer is simple. By intensifying the characteristics we want, inevitably, undesirable characteristics will emerge which have lain dormant in this exclusive stock. So we learn from experience that in-breeding diminishes the success of breeding sound stock in a long-term breeding programme. The breeder may decide to cull drastically, but there are conditions such as hip dysplasia, epilepsy, eye and mouth problems that may only manifest themselves long after the offspring have left the nest.

An alternative to in-breeding could be out-crossing – mating unrelated parents – which means that the offspring have a mix of different characteristics. So, having decided not to breed incestuously, why don't we out-cross repeatedly to encourage an ever-increasing richness in the array of characteristics? The answer is that we are unable to predict with any accuracy the vast complexities of introducing an unending stream of new genes for years to come. It would inevitably mean that the stock would fundamentally alter, losing type, and eventually bearing little likeness to the breed we wish to perpetuate.

There is an another choice, a compromise, to help us with our dilemma. This is the play-safe programme, which is a modification of in-breeding. The principle is to mate family-related dogs, but using dogs which are not too closely related. The object of this is to intensify the best characteristics of family type, and then out-cross once for desirable distinguishing traits, going to a dog who is also line-bred of strong family type. Thus, by taking time selecting and breeding from the type established, and then, every now and then, out-crossing to an animal of similar type but with new bloodlines, new genes can be brought to the pool. Lastly, the bitch contributes one half of the chromosomes that carry the genetic material, and the stud the other half, determining the characteristic of each puppy.

There are many books written on the science of genetics; I have touched on the simplest application concerning breeding dogs, and Vizslas in particular, one which many of us follow. Sometimes it succeeds and sometimes it does not, but then we are dealing with many imponderables. The tragedy is that, however well intentioned and ambitious the breeder may be, the full nature of the gene is not known. The rule of breeding excellence to excellence is fine in theory, but impossible to practise. The thousands of characteristics that must be taken into account means that there is no perfect dog.

It is important to remember that the Hungarian Vizsla started at a disadvantage in Britain. The first two imports, brother and sister, were inter-bred. Some of their offspring were inter-bred also – some of which were exported to America. Count Bela Hadik stressed this point in an article he wrote on the history of the breed: "All registered Hungarian Vizslas descend from seven or eight dogs in Hungary. It is apparent that twice within a reasonably short period, around 1918 and again around 1944, a certain amount of in-breeding became necessary to maintain the Vizsla breed. All Vizslas are therefore already fairly closely related. It is this fact which causes me to strongly oppose any further in-breeding."

Chauncey Smith gives his principal breeding guidelines, stating: "I believe that breeding plays a major role in the development of a good bird dog. I have always liked to say: 'Breed to the best and hope for the best.' Also: 'What you see is what you get.' Parents and grandparents play a major role. They feed into the equation by what you see is what you get. I also believe that in five generations you can breed the hunting desire out of most lines."

THE PRACTICALITIES OF BREEDING THE BITCH

There are a number of questions the potential breeder needs to ask himself, as the owner of a potential brood bitch. In European countries such as Germany and Switzerland, breeding is monitored by a breed master, and there is a committee that makes the decision as to the merits of a bitch. In Britain and in America there is no such system; the owner can be the sole arbiter. Therefore you must decide: what kind of breeder would you wish to be?

Do you fall into the category of the pet breeder, wishing to satisfy your own, and your bitch's maternal instincts, or attempting to provide fun for the children? Do you see yourself earning a bit of pin money, or making breeding a commercial venture? Are you someone who is dotty about the breed and wishes to see everyone owning a Vizsla? Or do you want to be a breeder who loves and knows the breed well, its faults and its merits, and likewise what sort of home would suit a puppy best? Are you objective enough to know whether your bitch can contribute to the gene pool? Let us look at the next step from the point of view of Time, Space and Finance.

Time

Whelping a bitch and caring for her offspring, is a non-stop job if the puppies are to reach their full potential. All the time in the world is needed to enjoy, cherish and nurture them. From the time the bitch starts to whelp, it is an unknown factor as to how well she will take to her maternal duties. Until the last puppy has packed his bags, it is a period of extreme hard work, and for the puppies these weeks are a vital time for socialising and relating to the first human in their life.

Space

The dam needs to have a quiet place where she can whelp and feed her brood in warmth and peace. As they grow, the puppies require an enclosed safe area where they can move about when they have outgrown the whelping box. As they begin to feel their strength, they need an area big enough to romp and play. At this stage – at five to six weeks of age – a litter of Vizslas is no longer that enchanting mass of sleeping russet-gold creatures; they are rumbustious, demanding young Vizslas, whose teeth are needle-sharp and whose appetites should be insatiable. They can escape from anything into everything. So, properly prepared facilities will mean peace of mind, and rearing will be an enjoyable experience. It is necessary to be prepared for the odd puppy to remain unsold until it is three to four months old – a sobering thought, but one that needs to be addressed. Equally, you must consider the possibility of having to take back a puppy if it does not suit its new home. It is vital that a breeder takes responsibility for his actions, for it is the breeder who chooses to bring puppies into the world.

Finance

Let us take into account some of the essential items necessary before and after the birth. These include: the stud fee, petrol (for travelling to and from the stud dog), a whelping box, an infra-red lamp, floor covering, food for the dam, food for the puppies, vet's bills, plus your time. It sounds straightforward enough to calculate the cost, but the unknowns can be crippling financially. If the vet is needed for the bitch or a sick puppy, or if a caesarian is necessary, the bills can mount up. Normal post-whelping vet's costs include removal of dewclaws and tail docking, a worming programme and inoculations. But nothing can be counted on, and costs will not be covered if there are few whelps and a sick dam.

Having satisfied yourself that you can manage all these contingencies, if they occur, it is time to look at the pros and cons of breeding from your bitch and which stud is to be chosen. The only way a novice can assess this is to consult a breeder, look at the breed, and study the Breed Standard. You must look at your bitch objectively, without rose-tinted spectacles, and then, knowing her faults and her qualities, you will need to find a stud dog with similar good characteristics, with a particular merit that may be an improvement on your bitch. Have a clear objective, and remember that breeding a mediocre animal to a mediocre animal only breeds mediocrity. It is not advisable to breed from a bitch before she is two years old. A Vizsla is hardly mature enough – physically or mentally – before this age, nor is it sensible to breed from her for the first time after five years of age. Of course, there are always exceptions, but these are acceptable guidelines. A bitch should never be bred from at every season: bearing puppies pulls a bitch down and she needs time to recover, to gain muscle and to enjoy a carefree period in her life.

THE BITCH IN SEASON

The Vizsla bitch should come 'on heat', or 'in season', for the first time at nine months of age or thereabouts. From then on, her cycle may be every six, nine or even twelve months. By the time she is ready to be bred from, her cycle will be established. The Vizsla is fastidious; she usually keeps herself very clean. Some bleed profusely and others hardly show at all. Some swell grossly, others remain tight until the time of mating. This does not mean to say that the season is not normal, nor does the ability to conceive seem to be affected.

The duration of her season, counting from the second day of showing, is twenty-one days. There are particular days during this period when the bitch ovulates, which is the time when she is ready to be mated and to conceive. This time usually starts from the tenth day and lasts to the twelfth, thirteenth or fourteenth day, possibly longer. There are many variables, but if the bitch constantly sits down or snaps at the male, this is a strong indication that she is not ready, or that her ovulation has finished. When she comes into season her discharge will be deep red; as it turns to a pale pink she is more likely to be ready to mate. It has been known for a Vizsla bitch to ovulate as late as the twenty-ninth day; in this instance she was mated and had some fine puppies. I have known a bitch to be mated on the tenth day and to go on bleeding until the twenty-first day – and she had a large litter. Lastly, another bitch had a heavy dark-red bleed two days after being mated; the vet assured me that she was most unlikely to come into whelp, but she did, and had a litter of ten healthy puppies.

Once you have made your choice of stud dog, and the owner has agreed to the mating, there are further details to be agreed upon. There are certain ethics that have to be understood, for example:

1. It is the owner of the bitch who chooses the stud dog. A stud dog owner does not ask for a bitch to mate his dog.
2. It is the responsibility of the owner to take the bitch to the dog on the appropriate day.
3. It is the responsibility of the stud dog owner to organise and monitor the actual mating.
4. The stud dog owner can offer two matings. Some breeders recommend a second mating the following day or the day after that. This is in case the first mating has not taken, but it is not obligatory. In the event of a bitch not conceiving, a free service on her subsequent season can be offered, but neither is this obligatory.
5. Some breeders return the stud fee if the bitch does not conceive, although it is not obligatory.
6. The stud dog owner can be offered a puppy in lieu of payment.

There is another point that comes under Code of Ethics. The stud dog owner can be put in an embarrassing position if the bitch's owner cannot really make his mind up and also leads other stud dog owners to believe that their dog is to be used. It is tactless and hurtful; be open, explain why there has been a change of choice, and thus avoid any cause for stress.

THE ACT OF MATING

The Vizsla presents few problems as a stud dog, as long as he learns what it is all about as a youngster. If he has mated early on, when he is around twelve months of age, he will get the hang of it, and will never forget. If he is fortunate to be put to a bitch who has been mated before, she may flirt and egg him on, which will encourage him to overcome his gauche ineptness.

The Vizsla's temperament is such that he prefers to be independent. At all times the male needs to feel dominant and should be encouraged to do so. The role the humans play in supervising a mating should be as retiring and unobtrusive as possible. As always with this breed, if the handler becomes overbearing, interfering too much in the natural course of things, the Vizsla's self-esteem and self-regard wavers. He feels crushed and insecure, and expects to be chastised. Handled sympathetically, he gains confidence in the knowledge that his instincts are right, and that he can work things out for himself.

The stud dog 'stands' on his own ground, one reason being that it is familiar territory. Always use the same area for mating, so he learns that 'this is where he mates'. I prefer the Vizslas to mate outside: they are free to run and play in natural surroundings. I believe that nature should take its course, and I only hold the bitch's head when the dog mounts her. This is so she cannot turn on him or move away, which could harm the dog at this point. In conclusion, if the Vizslas clearly do not wish to mate, my philosophy is to call it a day. I do not like forced matings. There are many types of stud dog. The handler must learn to accept each individual's style and to trust him. Some have a macho swagger – they burst out of the kennel, scarcely acknowledge the bewildered female, mate her, and that's it. Others need time before they can be relied upon to mate every bitch that is presented. Some never seem to show much enthusiasm, but eventually manage it. Others, perhaps more like the Vizsla we all know, are a little diffident at first. However, once the male has sniffed around and recognised that the bitch is ready, the Vizsla's gentleness and sweetness, dare we say romanticism, is often demonstrated while courting in the early stages. He likes to flirt and play, and he likes the bitch to flirt too. He can be easily put off by a bitch who is bad tempered, but as he becomes more confident, his determination and stubbornness will override all else. This characteristic is demonstrated so often in the Vizsla's make-up; once its shy naivety goes, it is a dog with drive and determination. I do believe that one of the reasons the Vizsla is a difficult dog to 'suss out', is its ability to lapse from great confidence to a subordinate, servile role and back again within a short space of time. This gives the impression that it's not so much the owner that does not understand, rather it is a breed that has problems in coming to terms with its own character.

The bitch produces a chemical known as pheromone in her urine when she is in season; it is this scent that the dog receives which arouses him sexually. When she is ready to mate with the dog, she will 'stand', presenting her enlarged vulva, with her tail twisted to one side. She is then ready to receive him (a bitch will never allow a dog to mate her unless she gives consent, and that is only when she is in season). He will mount her, clasping her round the hips with his front legs, holding her flanks steady. He searches for the entrance of her vulva with his erect penis. If he is inexperienced, he may have difficulty, but left alone he will usually manage perfectly well. It is at this stage that some handlers start to interfere. It can happen that the dog spends himself a little in his excitement, but as likely as not, this will only be a few drops of no consequence. When he does find the entrance his hind legs will make rapid jerking movements, getting a good grip on the ground in order to make complete penetration. Ejaculation takes place, and the prepuce or the foreskin of his penis will have been pushed back, and the swollen, bulbus glandis will be held by a restricting band of muscle of the vagina. It is this band of muscle that releases the penis to end the mating. Until it does, neither dog nor bitch can separate; this is known as the 'tie'. The tie may last from ten minutes to an hour. I have known it last an hour, and I must say that by then, doubts were beginning to flit through my mind: "suppose they don't separate!" But I was the only one having anxious thoughts, the mating pair had practically dozed off. Once the dog is released, the bulbus glandis reduces to normal and a small amount of fluid may be lost as the bitch moves away, but this is perfectly normal.

Through experience, I have learned that every mating is different. If the stud dog, for some reason, has not had a tie, or on occasion, if the bulbus glandis swells outside the bitch, and he has not entirely entered her, some semen may still find its way into the bitch and she may still conceive. If the male does ejaculate outside her and the bulbus glandis is swollen, it can be extremely uncomfortable for the dog, especially if it starts to dry, so quietly lead him away where he can sort himself out on his own, and everything will be packed away again.

It is of the utmost importance, especially when Vizslas mate, to remember that they are animals; it is a dangerous habit to give them human feelings. Close as we are to this affectionate breed, and as much as they empathise with us, it is their world and we must leave them to it, if they are to be dogs in their own right.

THE EXPECTANT MOTHER

The date of mating to the date of birth is sixty-three days; a couple of days either way is not unusual. During the gestation period no greater mistake can be made than to over-cosset and pamper the Vizsla bitch, or she will reflect the owner's anxiety. For the first three to four weeks after mating, she should be treated as usual, with the same exercise and feeding routine. At approximately the fifth week there are usually outward signs of the bitch being in whelp. Her nipples will redden and enlarge, and her belly will show signs of swelling. If she is clinging, fatter and doe-eyed, it may be that the owner's attitude has changed toward her and she is being paid more attention and fed the odd titbit here and there!

After the fifth week the protein value of the bitch's food should be increased. She will also need extra vitamins – but be advised by your vet at this point. Her food should be divided into two meals a day, as time goes on, and then three meals. As her pregnancy continues, the extra demands of the whelps within her increase, so it is vital for their welfare that she has the very best, but remember that a fat bitch is an unhealthy one. The final proof of a dam's pregnancy is the amazing sight of the puppies moving within her whilst she is lying peacefully on her side. This may be about three weeks before they are due.

It is as well to be prepared for any eventuality. In the wild a bitch hides herself and her puppies to obliterate any trace that they have been born; this is the only defence she has against an enemy. Her chosen place to whelp would have a small entrance, opening into a chamber, just large enough for her. The roof would be low, and the light would be subdued, the atmosphere damp and humid, and so we need to recreate an atmosphere for her that will give her a similar sense of security. Even the most civilised and gregarious bitch becomes primitive, to some extent, at whelping time. The degree varies, but it is always there. We must remember that this is also a confusing time for the bitch; she may not know exactly what she wants – either to be with people as in her normal life, or to seek seclusion. If the whelping box can be placed in a quiet, dimly lit room, preferably beneath a table or a low shelf she will feel safe and secluded. I enclose the front with a blanket over a clothes horse, which can be as movable as necessary. However, the bitch will probably be reluctant to stay there until she actually starts to whelp, although in principle this is where she should sleep, in order to get used to it. But often it does not work out that way. When one of my bitches is in whelp she will usually sleep in the bedroom – that way I can keep an eye on her; she is happy, and so am I. Thus, when her time comes – and it is always when the household has settled down for the night – we both move down to the whelping room. She can manage the birthing process perfectly, if she is safe in the knowledge that her owner is nearby.

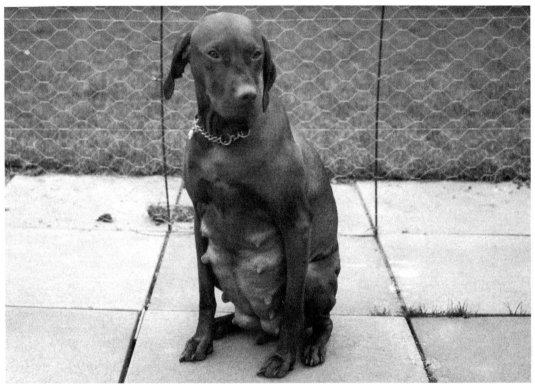

The expectant mother, a day before whelping. Lutra Golden Mystery. Owned and bred by S. Millson.   *Millson.*

ITEMS NECESSARY FOR WHELPING

1. Whelping box.
2. Infra-red lamp.
3. Newspaper.
4. Plastic rubbish bags.
5. Towels for humans, whelps, and dam.
6. Flannel and bowl of warm water for wiping bitch down.
7. Flannel, soap and bowl of warm water for washing hands.
8. Scissors for cutting umbilical cords.
9. Cotton wool (cotton).
10. Clock for noting times of deliveries.
11. Scales, pen and paper for weighing and recording birth-weights.
12. Drink for dam.
13. Chair and soft matting – kneeling can be hard on the bones!

THE WHELPING BOX

The whelping box should be large enough for the bitch to lie comfortably, and the front should be the correct height so the bitch and whelps can be tended easily. The front should also be removable to facilitate access while whelping is in process; it can be replaced once the whelping is over. Later on, when the pups are about four to five weeks old and are ready to venture in and out of the box to a play area, it can be removed again. The box should have shelves or a pig rail running all the way round the inside at a certain height. This provides shelter for a tiny whelp if the dam lies against the edge, its little body can roll to safety beneath the shelf. Later on, when the puppies are old enough to climb out of the box, the sides can be heightened by adding panels.

While the bitch is whelping, layers of newspaper are the most practical covering for the base. As the paper becomes soiled, it can be replaced. Once the puppies are born, a soft covering can be put down. There are several products on the market, all of which provide a warm, dry surface to lie on, and they can be washed in the washing machine. Some bitches continue to 'dig up' the box after the birth, and if the rugs are left loose a whelp could be suffocated beneath the folds. My latest discovery for fixing this floor covering to the base of the box, is to staple it down with a heavy-duty stapler.

An infra-red lamp is essential; it provides a constant source of warmth. If it is suspended to one side of the box, it enables the whelps and dam to lie beneath it, or away from the heat, if they wish. If puppies have to struggle to keep warm they have much less chance of thriving. The temperature in the room should be approximately 75 degrees Fahrenheit. The puppies may need the lamp for three to four weeks, depending on the weather.

PRE-BIRTH SIGNS

There are several distinct signs that the birth is imminent. If the bitch's temperature is taken for a few days towards the end of the gestation period, there will be a distinct drop as the whelps are due (normal temperature is 100 to 101 degrees Fahrenheit). This, coupled with loss of appetite, marked agitation and restlessness, and scraping up her bedding, are clear indications that her time is near. Lastly, there is a loss of sticky opaque fluid, 'the plug' or 'the breaking of the waters', indicating that the cervix is opening.

THE DELIVERY

As the first puppy moves down the birth canal, the bitch will try to lick her quarters, squat down, dig up the paper in her box and perhaps whine. When she starts to pant fiercely, gazing into the distance, the whelp is descending, one big push and the whelp has arrived. Sometimes the Vizsla bitch prefers to get out of the box, squat to have her puppy on the floor, and then return to the clean box with her newly born pup. At this stage there is nothing the owner can do but remain calm; a quiet voice and gentle reassuring presence will give her confidence. Let the birth be as natural as possible with the least obtrusive help.

Whelps usually arrive head-first, encased in a fine bag of membrane. The umbilical cord is attached to the placenta and as the whelp slips out, the dam will pull the membrane away, eating this, and the placenta, cleaning and licking her parts and the whelp with great intent. The whelp will lie inert; at this point it seems neither dead nor alive. It is crucial that the dam encourages it to breathe on its own for the first time. She will nick the cord cleverly, allowing exactly the right amount on to dry and eventually drop off. She will continue to lick the whelp vigorously from head to foot, to stimulate it to move. Then, with a little cry or flick of a leg, the whelp is taking its first breath. The bitch instinctively pushes it about with her nose, rolling it over quite roughly, until eventually she allows it to move toward her cornucopia, which will provide her nursling Vizsla with all the nourishment it will need for the next three weeks at least. The novice whelper will have learned, in the space of ten minutes, how strong the maternal instinct is in the Vizsla, and how strong and determined a whelp can be – survival is all. The new-born puppy suckles and clings to the nipple, once it has found it. As the newborn arrives it may be striped like a tiger. However, even though it is difficult to imagine, these markings will fade after a few days. Of course, things rarely go according to plan. A puppy may come out feet-first, it may arrive with no bag, with the umbilical cord already severed, or there may be no sign of the placenta. The 'whelper' may have to break the sac, and cut the cord, all in a matter of seconds, while the dam is busy with the afterbirth. This is not important, as long as the puppy is alive and well.

Let us consider the placenta for a moment; it has been each whelp's vital connection with its mother, through which nutrients, oxygen and much more are passed from the dam to the foetus. As the birth approaches, it degenerates and secretes a green fluid, which emerges from the bitch during the birth as a dark blood colour, staining a hectic green. It is full of rich nourishment. The bitch has an extremely strong instinct to eat it; seemingly, in the wild, she would have needed it for food, and would have removed it to hide all traces of the birth. It is not advisable to let the bitch eat all the afterbirths, as their richness can upset her after whelping. However, some bitches are so intent on disposing of the afterbirth that it can be quite a tussle who will get there first.

Further contractions will herald another whelp; and so the exciting process continues. The dam will settle down, cleaning and feeding, in between delivering whelps. If they do not come too quickly, she has a chance to rest and organise herself. If she has a wide birth-canal, her new-born will arrive with three or four good, effective contractions, which will not tire her. It is shallow, ineffective contractions that do little to initiate the birth process, and this proves extremely tiring for the mother. She can become very distressed if there is something amiss, and if she continues for more than two hours in this manner it is best to call the vet.

As the number of whelps increases, and each new birth is imminent, the puppies can be put beneath the lamp, while their mother concentrates on the new arrival. A bitch can become very distressed if the puppies are removed while the whelp is arriving, which is sometimes advised; it is far better not to give her any cause for anxiety at this time. If a whelp sounds a little bubbly in the chest, the fluid that is present needs to be removed. This can be done by holding it upside down, and cleaning the mucus from its mouth. The whelp may also need help to feed at first, just until it gets the feel of the nipple in its mouth. This should be done by holding the nipple in the left hand, and slipping the forefinger of the right hand in the corner of the puppy's mouth; as it opens, squeeze the nipple in, and at the same time milk will drip. Once the whelp latches on, it will get the idea!

As the quiet hours pass by, the puppies will feed and sleep, making little whelp noises of contentment. A dozing brood bitch will reassure you that all is well. At some time she will need to be taken outside, on a lead, to relieve herself. She will be reluctant to leave her little ones, but it will do no harm. It may also prove that she has another whelp tucked up somewhere. Frequently, when she seems to have finished whelping and there are no more lumps to be felt, she produces another one after moving about. It is always advisable to have the vet see the bitch and puppies after the whelping appears to have been completed. But even a vet can be fooled! After the birth of eleven puppies, when the vet had checked that all was well, I waved goodbye to him at the gate, the dam standing proudly by my side; then she popped back into her puppies – and then there were twelve!

Future Vizsla owners often ask: "Which do you prefer, bitches or dogs?" I do not have the answer; each Vizsla dog or bitch has its own specific role and character, and has a different place in my heart. But it is very memorable to be part of the experience of whelping a bitch. We allow dogs into our world, but at this time we are permitted into theirs – as the bitch stirs to touch each puppy with her nose, settles an errant whelp who has ventured too far from her, and lies back gazing at her brood adoringly, ever caring, ever watchful. She looks up, secure and content, her tail thumps in recognition and appreciation, and then she returns her attention, in utter devotion, to her whelps, totally accepting motherhood.

WHELPING DIFFICULTIES

Times to call the vet

1. Uterine Inertia
When the bitch does not produce contractions.

2. Eclampsia
The symptoms are shuddering, great agitation and panting. This can be partly due to insufficient absorption of calcium. This condition must be treated immediately. It may occur before whelping or during, but is most likely three weeks after the puppies are born.

3. A whelp's position
A whelp may be positioned in the birth canal in such a way that contractions are not sufficient to expel it. It is advisable to call in a professional.

If there are any deformed puppies in the litter, obviously it is advisable to put them down; but even though a large litter presents difficulties, as long as they are healthy and vigorous, they should be given the right to live. It will be more work for the owner and for the bitch, but a bitch handles a litter of eleven or twelve if she is fit and healthy. The puppies can be weaned earlier than a small litter, with no ill effect.

FEEDING THE DAM

A bitch feeding five puppies may need to take in four times her normal ration during the time the puppies are making the heaviest demands on her. High protein diet is essential, so plenty of fresh meat should be added to her normal diet. Most bitches look in wonderful health during their pregnancy, but after whelping, for a period, they look in very poor condition, and for the first few days after whelping they pant and fuss, but after that they settle into a rhythm of sleeping, feeding and caring. It is not necessary to give milk to the bitch in order that she produces milk – that is an old wives' tale. So too is the opinion that the poor bitch must be starved, in order for her milk to reduce and dry up when the time comes for the puppies to be weaned.

Chapter Seven

REARING THE LITTER

PATTERN OF DEVELOPMENT: (From Birth to Twelve Weeks)

Eyes open: Seven to ten days.
Stand upright: Three weeks.
Walk and run: Four weeks.
Baby teeth: Twenty-one days.
Balance on their own for urine and bowel movement: Three to three and a half weeks.
Body twitching during sleep: disappears by four weeks.
Ears developed: About fourteen days. Hearing acute about five weeks.
Barking: About eighteenth day.
Early play movements: Eighteen to twenty days.
Eat from dish: Three weeks.
Vigorous play among pups: Three and a half to four weeks.
Pecking order established within litter, personalities begin to emerge: Four to five weeks.
Play with toys: Five weeks.
Play constructively with litter mates, hiding, chasing: Five weeks.
Learning mouth and paw skills, body control: Five to six weeks.
Able to sleep continuously through night, e.g. 11pm-7am: Ten weeks.
Voluntary control of urination and defecation: Begins about twelve weeks, perfected from five to six months.

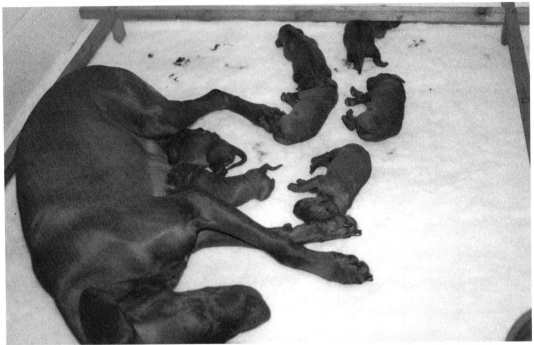

Lutra Golden Mystery and her two-day-old puppies. Owned and bred by S. Millson.

THE LITTER DEVELOPS

Healthy whelps are quiet, sleepy, warm, round, firm and plump. The skin and mucous membranes are pink, and a fold of skin collapses as soon as you let it go, as it does in all healthy dogs. Poorly puppies are limp when they are picked up. They have wrinkled, cold skin which feels damp. They squirm and cry constantly or lie cold and inert. It is hard to believe that the obsessively caring dam will leave a sick whelp alone, out in the cold, but in fact, she leaves it to die.

For the first three weeks the puppies feed and sleep. They are born with certain patterns, but they can neither see, hear, nor walk, and they are not able to urinate or defecate without the dam's stimulation. The dam will keep both the puppies and the whelping box spotlessly clean, until the litter is ready to be weaned. By the end of the third week the whelps make enormous strides. The brain, which is inactive at birth, develops rapidly, and from the twenty-first day the puppy's environment starts to shape its entire life, its intelligence and its emotions. This little being will start to relate to all that is going on around it. This is a time when a pup can become extremely upset, and it cannot adjust to great change, as it will do in two weeks time. I have often observed that contented puppies in the whelping box become extremely disturbed if it is opened up; clearly they are not ready for the outside world. But when they start trying to climb out, and then the whelping box is opened up, they welcome the extension of their freedom.

The puppies at a week old.

The litter at nineteen days. the dam will keep the puppies and whelping box clean.

Sh. Ch. Russetmantle Ochre's puppies at four weeks, now inquisitive about their environment.

TAILS AND CLAWS

Tails should be docked and dewclaws removed when the puppies are three to four days old. This is not for cosmetic reasons but for necessity. We have learned that those who first brought the Vizsla to Britain and America wanted it as a useful working dog. It adapted well to the different types of countryside, particularly to working thick cover. Once the Vizsla has reached its full potential it will face any type of cover. However, a handler would be reluctant to attempt to send a Vizsla into dense bramble or blackthorn, if it was to come out torn and bleeding, and this occurs if the tail is not docked. It is certainly better to dock at three to four days old than to have a dog's tail damaged and then amputated under anaesthetic when it is older.

It is also necessary to keep the puppies' nails short; they grow rapidly to become as sharp as needles. Some brood bitches do not seem sensitive to their puppies' scratches, but others will reach the stage when they cannot bear the puppies, and will refuse to get into the box with them. The golden rule is to trim the nails, little and often, using nail scissors.

WEANING AND FEEDING

Weaning is a crucial time for a litter. It needs the utmost care to make sure that it is not traumatic for the puppies. One way to avoid this is to stick to a routine, and to have food well prepared in advance – screaming, hungry puppies cause havoc. Give one new feed at a time; as soon as it is established that the food has not caused upset tummies, then it is safe to introduce another new item of food. If they are given too much variety to begin with, there is no way of knowing which new food is causing the upset.

The puppies will be ready to be weaned when they are three weeks old. It is at about this time that the mother will regurgitate her food for them; a strong indication that she knows they are ready for solid food, even though she has plenty of milk. I follow her example by giving the puppies solids first, while she continues to feed them their milk feeds. I make sure that the food is the same consistency and temperature as the bitch's digested, regurgitated food. When the pups graduate to two meat meals a day, the bitch's milk starts to diminish because there is less demand on her, and by that time the puppies readily take to milk feeds.

THE METHOD

To give the puppy the idea of chewing and eating instead of sucking, roll a small amount of raw finely chopped beef into a ball in the palm of your hand. Sit the pup on your knee, and hold the morsel of meat in the right hand. The puppy will take time, at first, until it gets the idea. This is its first venture on its own, and how it reacts to the experience will give the breeder quite a bit of information concerning its character. Does it seem timid? Does it gather confidence? Is it a good eater? Does it concentrate? Observing these early behaviour patterns will give clues to its needs, even at this age. After the puppy has had its first taste of meat, put it back to feed from the dam. This will help it to settle.

Give the puppies the same routine the following day, and if all is well, try cooked finely chopped beef and a complete food the following day, ensuring that it is mushed to resemble the dam's regurgitated food. Feed it in a shallow bowl on the floor – use two or three bowls if necessary – and observe closely. If one or two puppies are not interested, urge them a little, by putting some food on your finger and letting the pup lick it off. Allow the dam to go back in with the puppies to feed them afterwards. Increase these two feeds as the weeks go by, and, as long as there are no tummy upsets, you can feed chicken, tripe, and fish, as well as beef. When these meals are well established, introduce a milk and cereal meal in the morning, following the same principles, until the litter is well established on one milk, one meat, one milk and one meat feed, four times a day, four hourly. Meanwhile, gradually keep the dam away from the litter after feeds. By this time she will probably be heartily sick of them! As they grow on, the dam can find them very demanding, and it is quite distressing to see her mauled by her young ones. Sometimes a bitch will refuse to go into her puppies once they start being weaned, feeling her maternal duties are over. Somehow she realises that they are no longer dependent on her. She will happily see them off to their new homes without a backward glance. Now she can return to gentle exercise, and if she has a swim each day, all the better. It will help her to muscle up again, and her under-carriage will soon disappear.

By seven weeks the puppies will be on four meals a day. For example:

8am: Cereal and milk (I use a milk powder specially formulated for puppies).
12 noon: Minced cooked meat and complete food (soaked).
4pm: Rice pudding and milk.
8pm: Minced cooked meat and complete food (soaked).

The litter should always be offered water, but it is not advisable to leave it down, as they may also like to play with it! Puppies can be given large biscuits to gnaw, but not in between meals or their appetite will be blunted, so late evening may be the best time. They should also be on extra vitamins and they should have been wormed, starting at four weeks old, and continuing every two weeks. My vet recommends this programme until they are a few months old. But it is always a good idea to have a new puppy looked over by the vet, and he will give his own advice on these issues.

When the puppies are ready to go to their new homes, a diet sheet should go with them. If this is adhered to, even for the first week or two, the settling in period will be much less traumatic. A new home and a tummy ache is a lot to cope with at seven weeks old.

CHOOSING A VIZSLA PUPPY

The Vizsla puppy should be sturdy and strong; even at seven or eight weeks old it should look in proportion and compact. Its chest should be well down to its elbows; even at this stage it should look broad. If it has a bad front, elbows flapping, bowed legs and flat feet, this spells a problem for the future. If the pup looks high on the leg with rather light bone, this is unlikely to change. When you look at a puppy at ten to twelve weeks old, it can be that nothing looks right; every part of the pup can look out of proportion, with the exception of a good shoulder and rear angulation, which remain apparent. However, as the puppy matures, its good outline reappears. It needs to have rather strong, thick legs and knobbly wrist joints – these are growing points. A smooth knee at this stage means it has little growing to do. The head should be in proportion with the body, appearing neither too large and heavy, nor too small and narrow. In profile, the muzzle should not look tapered; it should look squared at the end. A small light-boned little specimen will not develop good strong bones, nor will a large heavy-bodied puppy with thick bone and bossy shoulders develop into a Vizsla who will fit the Breed Standard. The colour of the eyes changes, from blue when born, to green, to light brown, to hazel. Then if it is to be correct, the colour changes to a shade darker than the coat. It can take up to two years for the eyes to reach their true colour. The puppy coat will also take time to darken; the ears, the legs and the topline will darken up first, giving some indication of its eventual colour. But the pedigree will give a truer indication of the probable eye and coat colour, since both are inherited. For example, if a line is known for light, ginger or dark coats, it is likely the progeny will inherit the same colour, and similarly the eventual eye colour.

Duncarreg Sea Wren at seven weeks. Bred by B. Bugden. The Vizsla puppy should be sturdy and strong; it should look in proportion and compact.

Gardenway Red Admiral at ten weeks. Bred by J. Perkins. The Vizsla puppy needs to have stong, thick legs and knobbly wrist joints – these are growing points.

Russetmantle Marsh at three months. Owned by P. Hay. The muzzle should look squared, and the head in proportion with the body.

A Vizsla puppy should be bold, lively, exuberant and playful; its nose should be in everything, and it should walk toward its owner with tail wagging, showing confidence and pleasure. The fire-cracker puppy, that is nervy and excitable, or the shy, retiring pup is not typical of the breed. Chauncey Smith looks for a bold out-going puppy, but he adds that the puppy that is bold this week may not be the boldest next week. That is the one reason why he relies heavily on the breeding stock.

For a breeder this is also a critical time. For those who care deeply for the breed and for the puppies brought into the world, all the dreams and fantasies are slowly becoming a reality. There is nothing more thrilling than pairing up the owner and puppy, and to see they enchant each other. It is a good start for a little Vizsla and its owner, who will share the next twelve to fifteen years together. Personally, I do not feel the breed is always ideal for an owner who has not had or been brought up with dogs, but there are definite exceptions. The Vizsla is sensitive and very intelligent; therefore the owner needs to accept that although the breed has the ability to learn and absorb very quickly, it can as quickly become upset if it is disciplined too harshly. The best manner to adopt is one of affection and firmness, plus

Ch. Gardenway Charlotte at sixteen weeks. Owned and bred by J. Perkins.
This puppy became one of the top winning bitches in the breed.

constant reinforcement that your love and praise is there to be had in abundance, in return for the dog's co-operation and obedience. However, if the dog feels that its owner does not know what it is about, it will take liberties: for instance, insisting on sitting on every adult's knee; this is fine for a puppy, but it is a different matter with a two-year-old dog. A Vizsla's dominating affection can take the family over. But if you over-dominate this dog, it becomes ashamed and chagrined. Once owner and dog come to an understanding, and a bond grows of mutual trust and respect, the dog will want to please, and that continues the conditioning process that it has been used to from a whelp of three weeks old.

Hopefully, the breeder will take great care counselling future owners, inviting them to visit the future dam, and the whelps at about three weeks old, or later when the puppies are running about. These visits are enjoyable occasions for the puppies and the visitors; the more socialising Vizslas can have at this stage the better. The breeder learns more of the life style and temperament of the future owners, which helps when it comes to assessing and matching puppy and owner. It is also advisable to encourage would-be owners to see the breed, especially as adults, in every aspect, before finally acquiring a puppy. This muscled, lively breed may not be what they want, or what they can cope with in their busy, regulated lives. A Vizsla is not the type to lie on the mat for too long; its vivacious temperament is much more "let's get up and go!".

So at seven weeks old the little Vizsla is ready to go; a week earlier it would have been too soon to leave the nest, but by now it cannot wait to be with humans – it wants all the spoiling it can get. It is ready to enjoy its new home; its feeding should be no problem, and its routine is well and truly established – and so its bags are packed. The puppy should leave the breeder with a diet sheet, details of its worming programme, its pedigree and its Kennnel Club registration form, if it has come through.

ARE YOU PREPARED ?

A puppy is bound to feel strange and uncertain in its new surroundings, but it soon learns its way about; where it eats, where it sleeps, and who to relate to. The pup needs warmth and affection, and will be desperately unhappy if it is left alone at first. Once it feels safe and secure, it won't mind nearly so much, but a Vizsla cannot tolerate being on its own for long. It is strictly a companion dog, who loves to be part of the family; it is not a solitary type at all. Vizslas are gregarious, and love nothing better than sharing their zest for living with the people in their lives.

One of the issues that occurs again and again is "Where does the puppy sleep?" It seems against many people's principles to allow the puppy to sleep in the obvious place, for the first few nights, which is in a bedroom where there is human company and security. If the puppy is put in the kitchen, in the dark, and alone, naturally it is going to cry, and it is going to relieve itself, out of fear and cold. So then the puppy will have to deal with an irate human in a dressing-gown, who is angry on two counts: firstly because the household cannot sleep, and secondly because the pup's house training has not got off to a very good start. Whereas, with a bit of lateral thinking, the little puppy sleeps warm and secure in its box, with humans nearby, and it does not stir until morning. After a few days you can take the box downstairs, and then if the puppy makes a fuss, it can be corrected and reassured by a firm voice from the human it has come to know and love, and who would do it no harm. The puppy's arrival is going to consume many hours of its owner's time until it is settled in, and this may take a couple of weeks. The pup will not need a walk for some time, but it can play outside, as long as it is an area which is not frequented by other dogs until it has had its inoculations.

HOUSE TRAINING

House training a Vizsla puppy is very easy, as long as the owner has a method, and it is better if one person is responsible for this task. The simplest method is to concentrate on conditioning the puppy to "go" outside, and not on the kitchen floor. If you encourage its cooperation with clear instruction and reward, the puppy will be happy to please you, once it understands what you wish it to do. A seven or eight week old Vizsla puppy cannot be house trained if there is a hint of punishment in the air.

The bladder is controlled by the sphincter muscle. As it fills with urine it reaches a certain point when the nerve supply to the muscle enables it to relax, and the bladder empties. Another set of muscles enable it to close. The nerves in the brain which control the functions of elimination are hardly developed until the puppy is five or six weeks old; it can then begin to learn to control the opening and closing of its bladder by conditioned reflex. This learning process can be interrupted by confusion and stress.

THE METHOD

Chose a spot outside where the puppy can "go", either a grassy patch or on soil. You will notice that it will always want to urinate and defecate after a meal, so pick the puppy up and put it down on its place, and once it goes there two or three times, it will get the message, especially if the word "Out" or something similar is used while it is actually 'in the act'. The pup will then associate the word with the deed. When it succeeds, give plenty of praise and make a fuss of it. Soon the puppy will start to go towards the door, and the next step will be that it will wait at the door asking to go out. At this stage both of you can feel very pleased. This combined effort is all part of bonding. If the puppy makes a mistake, pick it up firmly, take it out and put it on its place, saying, "Out". No punishment is necessary: by reinforcing the lesson again and again, you help the puppy to learn control. If it gets upset, as likely as not it will make a mistake because it has lost concentration and is feeling nervous.

Chapter Eight

CARING FOR YOUR VIZSLA

Over the years I have been involved with Vizslas, I have found that owners come up against the same problems, many of which relate specifically to the Vizsla. I have therefore highlighted the most common problems that arise, and provided some answers and solutions which, more often than not, seem to work.

EXERCISE

How much exercise does my Vizsla need?

The Vizsla is a dog which needs sensible exercise. Regular walks every day, where it can be free to stretch its legs, to play and search out scents, where it can feel independent. A Vizsla does not take kindly to being cooped up, nor to being left on its own. It will need good country walks, and whatever the weather, it loves being outside, but it also loves the family fireside. Treat your Vizsla sensibly; if it is happy, do not over-cosset; this dog is capable of working all day in the pouring rain and freezing weather.

A puppy needs gentle, playing exercise, but from the point of view of socialising, it needs to be taken out and about as much as possible. At no time should a puppy be allowed to tire or wear itself out. The bones are not fully formed, and a puppy can put too much strain on them, which will affect its conformation. A Vizsla can easily become over-excited; thus over-stimulation by throwing sticks or balls is not sensible. In all aspects, the Vizsla needs to be treated with respect, acknowledging its potential as a hard-working gundog; it only becomes an hysterical, stupid dog if humans make it so.

How much road-work should my Vizsla do?

If you show your dog, then, to achieve the highest possible muscle tone throughout, the type of exercise routine it has will be based on producing a fit dog, whose coat will gleam and who will be neither too fat nor too thin. Regular exercise for all Vizslas is essential. In this case, part of every walk should be on a hard surface, on the lead, with the dog walking or trotting with its head held up so that it is balanced. Choose a route where the dog can have half an hour on hard ground, and for the rest of the walk, it can be off the lead, enjoying itself.

If a dog is suffering from slack pasterns, loose elbows, flat feet, a poorly muscled neck, or if its quarters are weak, this exercise routine will tighten the muscles. If the dog's conformation is incorrectly constructed, little will change. Beware of over-doing road-work; it can be over-muscling. Give a puppy time to mature before attempting a rigid routine like this. If it has no faults in its construction, loose elbows and soft feet will naturally tighten as the puppy matures.

Can I exercise my bitch when she is in season?

Your Vizsla is safest indoors or in her kennel. Supervised exercise in a garden or yard is permissible, but remember: dogs in the area cannot be blamed for scenting a bitch on heat; they are reacting to instinct. Bitch owners must be responsible for restricting their animals during this time, and in that way no accidents will occur.

FEEDING

How much does an adult Vizsla eat?

It is difficult to state exact quantities. A sensitive owner will learn the right balance by looking at his dog. If your Vizsla is a little on the plump side, decrease the amount you are feeding, and vice versa. Much depends on the temperament of your Vizsla: some are picky eaters, and some cannot eat fast enough and are always asking for more. A balanced diet must include:

Protein – Essential constituent of muscle.
Carbohydrates – Provides food most rapidly converted to energy.
Fats – Burn more slowly than carbohydrates, and are thus a reserve fuel and a source of A and D vitamins, essential for sound bone and tissue structure.

Some owners only feed raw meat and biscuits, others use a complete food or scraps from the table. In order to have your Vizsla in top condition, making good bone from the beginning and reaching its full potential, it must be fed the best quality food. A Vizsla expends a high degree of energy, unlike a more lethargic breed, and therefore its body needs re-fuelling. For a young, active Vizsla I feed a complete food with cooked beef, chicken ox-cheek or tripe, and stock or gravy. I would want an adult to eat approximately 3lbs of complete diet and 3lbs of meat a day. An older Vizsla would not need so much, as it leads a more sedentary life. I feed twice a day on the basis that the gulpers will not have bloat problems, and the fastidious eaters will find smaller meals more appetising.

After whelping, a brood bitch is fed three or four times a day to keep the weight on. During the shooting season the dogs are fed extra meat plus larger feeds if they start to look ribby. If your Vizsla has an attack of diarrhoea or an upset tummy, and does not seem ill, you may find that a meal or two of boiled rice and chicken will solve the problem. Obviously, if the dog is running a temperature, call the vet.

What should I do with a puppy who will not eat?

A puppy who has been used to eating in competition with others in the litter is going to find it very strange adjusting to being the only one; it is fatal if the owner gets in a state as well. Allow the puppy time – I have never known a puppy refuse food for long. My advice is not to change the diet it has been used to for the moment; in fact sometimes the reason can be that the food tastes different or the consistency has changed or the temperature is wrong. Make sure you take notes from the breeder.

When the puppy is older, it may become bored with the same food, so keep the basic complete food, and chop and change the meat. The food may be too dry or too sloppy. Do not be tempted to leave food down or give the dog titbits, which will blunt its appetite. I cut out the milk feeds fairly soon, which means the puppy has more appetite for the two main meals. If a fat little puppy will not eat and is losing weight, and whatever you do makes no difference, try the following method, which I discovered quite by acccident, and it has proved invaluable. I had a puppy who so missed its littermates that it refused to eat food, or would only eat the minimum. One day I dropped a bowl of puppy food on the ground and the mushy contents lay in a heap; the puppy gobbled up the lot, having refused the same food in the bowl. From this moment it never looked back, but for quite a few weeks it ate in this way. This sometimes works for an adult too. I can only conclude that the puppy must have thought the mess on the floor was its mother's regurgitated food. I have also noticed that when a puppy is teething, it may go off its food; the gums can be very red and swollen, and most probably they feel sore.

How can I stop my Vizsla looking as thin as a rake?

If your Vizsla has lost weight, there are obvious causes you need to check:

1. Has the dog been wormed recently?
2. Is the dog running off weight by expending too much energy – you could be giving too much exercise?
3. Does the dog fret if there is a bitch in season in the area?
4. Is the dog ill?

All these are possible reasons why your Vizsla is looking ribby. But of course, if your dog is a picky eater it is a task to keep it looking fit; an inch of fat on or off this dog will show. Changing the diet may help, adding tasty gravy or a sprinkle of cheese. Add anything the dog fancies to its basic food. Chicken, lamb or tripe may tempt its palate. One of the cheaper canned dog foods, which contains a lot of fish seems to appeal when other foods are refused. Yeast or yeast tablets stimulate the appetite, and these are available from the chemist.

Once your Vizsla starts to eat, it is essential that it is fed regularly so that its system and its salivary glands become accustomed to anticipating mealtimes. Above all, and this is the most difficult thing to achieve, the owner must learn to accept the situation. Do all you can, but then you must leave the dog to do what it wants. If the dog is fussed or it feels your anxiety, matters will only get worse, because the dog will reflect your worry. If your dog continues to starve itself, take it to the vet for a check; animals rarely refuse to eat anything for long, unless they are sick.

BEHAVIOUR

How can I get my Vizsla to accept car journeys?

In general, most Vizslas love cars; a Vizsla would prefer to sit in the car than be left behind. It seems to regard the car as its own property when the owner is not there. The mildest of Vizslas will guard the car with his life!

Puppies are often sick in the car. A puppy of seven weeks, travelling for the first time, may not be so affected, but at twelve weeks it may be dreadfully upset. The older puppy's sense of awareness and fear are more developed in every way. If its feeling of giddiness and nausea become associated with your anger and apprehension and general turmoil, it will learn to hate the car. So try to avoid travel sickness by calmly taking the puppy for short rides at first, so that it gets used to the gentle motion of the car. Let the pup sit in the front, preferably being held steady by a passenger. If the puppy is in the back, the car's swaying can fling it off balance, and it is the constant change of balance that can cause discomfort. Never feed a puppy before a journey and take a towel, just in case! Drive to a location where the puppy can have a walk, or let the pup sit in the car at home, with its favourite chew, and then it will learn to associate the car with pleasure. In most cases, the puppy will soon grow out of car-sickness, but if it continues to have the problem, your vet may agree to give a tranquillizer, which may break the syndrome.

How do I stop my Vizsla getting out of hand?

The Vizsla's attractive puppyhood behaviour changes rapidly as it matures. A newcomer to the breed will find this difficult to believe until actually experiencing it; and certainly, first-time dog owners, without any knowledge of puppy training, may feel they have made a big mistake. This little puppy can develop into an unruly wilful dynamo. There are moments when it tears about the house, especially early in the evening when the family are wanting to settle quietly. The youngster becomes boisterously affectionate, over-demanding and defiant, jumping on chairs and leaping at people to greet them. In fact to be truthful, the dog is beginning to dominate the household in its wilfulness, and no-one is enjoying its presence as much as they were. This juvenile stage starts at about twelve weeks old and can continue until the dog reaches full sexual maturity. As it grows physically and mentally, not only is its muscular body fired with enormous energy, but so is its brain. The dog's adolescent growth and lack of mental discipline must lead to frustration. It is bred to be lively and to work; it is bred to perform specific disciplines which require a highly tuned brain. If the owner motivates himself to provide outlets, and the Vizsla is given a good, basic early training programme the Vizsla's normal adolescent behaviour will be modified, and its idiosyncracies will be but a passing phase.

How can I stop my Vizsla jumping up?

Many youngsters go through a period of grabbing hold of clothing or a hand; this is not an acceptable habit and needs to be curbed quickly. Puppies rarely grab each other, or their dam, causing pain. This is because they have learned that there will be retaliation, especially from the dam who will growl and push the puppy to the ground, holding its neck in her mouth, but without a scratch. There is no viciousness in this ritual. How does the human deal with the situation? In the same way. If the puppy grabs a hand with its needle-sharp teeth, immediately say "No", in a low growling voice, and push the puppy to the ground. If it stops, give plenty of praise, if it continues, repeat the discipline; the puppy has to learn – as it was taught by the dam – that there are limits. Similarly, if a puppy jumps up at people, this is totally unacceptable; it could push a child or an adult over if it is over-boisterous. Do not expect others to discipline your dog; it is your responsibility. Train your dog to sit by you, or at least stay to heel, if a visitor arrives. If the dog persists in jumping up, put it on a lead, and as it goes to jump up, give it a good yank, saying "No". Once the dog has got the message, continue to praise it for its good behaviour when your guests arrive. Continue to anticipate, and remind the dog, just in case it forgets, and before long you will be able to trust it completely.

Are Vizslas good with children?

Yes, in general they are. If they are brought up with children they learn to trust them, and adore their family. But if they have not been accustomed to children from puppyhood, they will be suspicious and fearful, as they would be of anything that seemed threatening to them – from umbrellas to cows. In this situation, most Vizslas would want to slink away and hide, but if a child persisted in seeking a dog out, it would retaliate with a warning growl.

Are Vizslas good with cats?

Again, the answer is yes, in general, and if a Vizsla is brought up with a kitten, the pair could become firm companions. A Vizsla is much more likely to be frightened of an aggressive cat. Dogs are brought up to respect cats in Britain; elsewhere, in Germany for instance, the Vizsla is encouraged to chase and retrieve cats to encourage its aggression.

Should I give my Vizsla a bone?

Dogs need a good chew on something hard. Bones help to keep the teeth and gums free from deposits of tartar, but they do produce strong primitive instincts. The dog naturally wants to keep a bone to itself, and will protect the bone fiercely if there is any threat of losing it. If a dog is to share the human environment it has to learn to adapt and moderate its behaviour. The dog must accept your dominance. I suggest you give your Vizsla puppy a bone, making sure that it has to give the bone up to you, if you say so.

There are dangers in giving a dog cooked bones. They can splinter and, of course, if the splinters are swallowed, they can cause great harm. An uncooked shin bone is chew-proof; even so, I have a Vizsla who eventually gnaws a bit off.

HEALTH CARE

Routine grooming, nail clipping, teeth cleaning, inspection of ears and eyes, should begin from puppyhood, so that being handled becomes second nature to the dog.

Do I need to I clip my Vizsla's nails?

The nails grow in a curve and, sooner or later, if they are not clipped, they will touch the ground. As the dog walks the long nails will force the toes and pads apart, causing discomfort and uneven and erratic movement. If the nails are kept short the pads will touch the ground first, and the muscles will keep the foot sufficiently tight to bear the dog's weight correctly.

Clip your Vizsla's nails with a standard nail-clipper; I prefer the guillotine type. I find the least traumatic method is to have my Vizsla sitting behind me on a large arm chair. The dog eventually learns that, come what may, and however long it takes, it will end up with its nails cut. I am firm but never angry; a dog hates to be held too tightly and the Vizsla is no exception. Slowly it dawns on the dog that it is not going to be hurt, and it might as well give in; the slightest acquiescence on the dog's part I reward with praise. After a few sessions even the most difficult dog comes to learn that the experience is not too unpleasant. If a nail has been cut too short and it bleeds, this shows the dog that it was right to be scared; so just take the tip of the nail off, and clip little and often, rather than be tempted to cut a chunk off.

The subject of nail-clipping is raised so often as a problem – and few dogs like having their feet handled. My conclusion is that they have tickly feet, and some more than others! I have yet to find a Vizsla who likes having its feet manicured!

How do I keep my Vizsla's teeth clean?

Clean teeth and healthy gums are important. As the Vizsla ages, deposits of tartar form, especially round the back molars. If the hard calculus is not scraped off it can cause soreness and deterioration of the gums. It can be scraped off with a dentist's scaling instrument, but routine cleaning, either with a toothbrush or cleansing with a swab dipped in salt solution, sodium bicarbonate or hydrogen peroxide, keeps the teeth fresh and clean. In some cases chewing or gnawing on a bone or hard biscuits etc. is sufficient.

Do I need to clean my Vizsla's ears?

The inside of the Vizsla's ears are hairless and it has few problems, generally. It is advisable to inspect and clean them, especially if you work your Vizsla – the flaps can get scratched and sore inside. Clean them off with a solution of witch hazel or olive oil on cotton wool (cotton) and apply an appropriate ointment. If the inner ear has accumulated wax and dirt, a twist of cotton wool dipped in a few drops of oil will soften it up, or a solution your vet has advised. Never poke about inside the ear with cotton-wool buds (cotton swabs); the convolutions of the ear could be damaged. If your Vizsla shakes its head and flaps its ears, it may have an irritation from mites or an infection, so it is advisable to consult your vet.

The Vizsla's ear tip may dangle in its food bowl when it is eating. This can cause hard lumps, that are crusted and dry, to cling round the edge. Do not be tempted to pick them off like a scab: the tender skin may bleed, causing further problems. Soften the crusts with a salt solution or oil and eventually you will be able to wipe them off.

Is there any special care needed for my Vizsla's eyes?

If the eyelids fit closely as the Breed Standard requires, there should be few problems. If there is a slight accumulation of mucus in the corners it should be removed by dipping a piece of cotton wool in a saline solution. Always slide the wool across the eye once and throw it away. Using a dirty finger or the same swab over again can cause and spread infection. If there is pus or discharge from the eye, be advised by your vet.
How do I keep my Vizsla's coat in good condition?

The Vizsla's smooth coat needs little attention, if the dog is healthy. Regular swimming will keep the coat clean and glossy; bathing and shampooing are hardly necessary. However, if you decide to bath your Vizsla, select a shampoo that will not dry its coat; the Breed Standard asks for a greasy coat for good reason. A rubber mitten is ideal to remove moulting hair and to tone the dog up. Then you can polish with velvet or silk and the coat will have a lustrous sheen!

Lastly, if your Vizsla's eyes are dull and its coat looks drab, its breath or ears smell, these are signs that the dog is out of sorts, so be advised by your vet. I have noticed that when the hair stands up in a dark ridge down the dog's back or its coat 'stares', there is usually something amiss.

Do Vizslas suffer from hereditary diseases?

The Vizsla is still small in numbers compared to some other gundog breeds, but every breed has its peculiar susceptibilities to hereditary diseases and faults. However, as far as can be assessed, a responsible watchfulness has been adopted to ensure the essential qualities of the breed are retained. Thus, the likelihood of hereditary faults and diseases becoming a major problem is reduced.

There are a number of conditions that have been observed and continue to be monitored in the breed:

1. Hip Dysplasia: Improper bone formation in the hip joints. Many more Vizsla owners now take advantage of the hip scoring scheme, and the hip score averages show the breed is in a healthy state.

2. Entropion: The lower eyelid does not fit tightly and curls inward, causing pain and irritation.

3. Tail Deformities: Either crooked, bent or stubbed.

4. Epilepsy: Spontaneous release of nervous impulses from within the brain leading to fits, varying in intensity from a fleeting disturbance of consciousness to a fully fledged convulsion.

5. Haemophilia: A blood disorder.

6. Mouth Malformation: Undershot Bite – when the lower jaw protrudes beyond the upper. Overshot Bite – when the upper jaw protrudes over the lower.

7. Skin Rash: One or two whelps or the whole litter at 3 to 4 days old can develop spots, varying from one or two tiny ones to large scabby areas. It is believed that the whelp's

immune system cannot deal with mites that are normally in the hair follicles. Once the system has adjusted, the problem should disappear. However, if the spots become infected, the condition must be treated.

Finally it must be taken into account that defects and diseases are not always hereditary, and it is essential to eliminate other causes such as injury, infection, poisoning and stress. In order to go forward in organising an effective breeding programme, facts and statistics are vital; hearsay is not scientific and therefore it is worthless.

Chapter Nine

THE PRINCIPLES
OF TRAINING

EARLY LEARNING

NATURE AND NURTURE

Inheritance of certain traits has a strong influence on behaviour, but it is the interaction of inherited and environmental factors that finally determines the behaviour of the mature dog. A pedigree can be well endowed with working and Champion Vizslas, indicating inherent good looks and sound working ability; but at critical stages in the Vizsla's early puppyhood, it can be so affected by lack of socialisation and deprivation of emotional attention, that it can never achieve its full potential. A shy, unpredictable or over-aggressive Vizsla is just as likely to have been affected by its environment early on as by its bloodlines.

I am starting this section on training by calling it 'Early Learning' for the simple reason that from the time a puppy is old enough to respond to its surroundings, at three weeks old, it is being conditioned to learn, to be taught, or trained – whatever word we wish to use. Everything the dog learns is by association of ideas and example; if it gets the wrong impression, it is difficult, if not impossible, to eradicate. The learning process continues throughout the dog's active life, but it is never so receptive as it is in its first few months. A Vizsla who has had a wide range of experiences during its formative period will be motivated to seek out a more enriched environment; it will be easier to train and its temperament will be more reliable. An innately shy dog will tend to avoid new experiences by withdrawing from everything. In a self-restricting environment, it will learn little, and will develop few new associations.

There is a magical moment when a puppy, still in the whelping box, first focuses on you. It looks at you, maybe but a fleeting contact, but it registers. Then comes the delightful stage when a puppy detaches itself from the warm heap of russet-golds, and makes a move towards you. It looks, it hears, and it responds to your eyes, face and voice by walking forward, wagging its tail. These are the first moments of bonding with a human. It only takes two or three days for a puppy to get its act together, and soon it hears your voice, recognises the face, associates the two, and totters as fast as it can towards you, wagging its tail in pleasure. The puppy will then want to be picked up, associating you with pleasure. The way in which the human responds and continues to imprint, will affect the puppy deeply.

During the weaning period the puppy is also learning to be handled. It becomes accustomed to being picked up and moved away from its warm siblings, but its feeling of distress and isolation can be quite acute. You are the human who comforts and feeds; its transference is natural, if it is made as easy as possible. The puppy will quickly become accustomed to the assertion of the humans in its home. Cutting nails and worming can be quite traumatic experiences, but handled firmly and kindly, the puppy learns control and trust, and it learns that firmness and kindness go hand in hand. It also learns that it can now feel secure with a human, as well as in its whelping box world. Thus, its attachments become more diverse.

Hands play a very significant role in the puppy's life, but never more so than now. Hands fondle and stroke in a gentle manner, they discipline by their strength, they can be dominating or submissive. They feed and nurture, comfort and chastise. Firm hands tell the puppy that it is secure and safe; they teach the pup to play and try its strength. It learns to trust these loving hands and the person they belong to. If those hands are harsh or heavy, imparting messages of rejection, callousness or coldness – hands that slap and push away – the Vizsla will also learn to avoid and reject the person they belong to – and other humans too, if it has learned repeatedly that this is how a human behaves. The puppy becomes people-shy and introverted; it will take it a long time to learn to trust, if ever.

READY TO LEAVE THE NEST

A critical time of the Vizsla's life is the period when it leaves all that it has known so far. This is a time of great transition; but if the puppy has had a solid upbringing, it will be ready to leave its litter brothers and sisters. At seven or eight weeks a puppy needs and demands individual attention. It does not want to share a human, it wants its own, and what could be better than a family that is ready to lavish it with loving care. The puppy will have its own food bowl, its own basket, its own blanket; it is ready to be a Vizsla in its own right.

At the weaning stage, the puppy's mother provided security; this role is taken over by the breeder, and now, at seven weeks, the breeder awards the new owner the responsibility for the puppy's welfare. The puppy does not need cosseting; its education can progress in the context of security. It needs to learn the house rules and boundaries, and it should be ready to enjoy all the comings and goings of a busy household. The Vizsla is a lively, vital, curious and intelligent breed, and almost in spite of itself, it cannot help but put its nose into everything. With strangers or strange situations a typical Vizsla puppy will hesitate to begin with, go forward with its tail down, then its tail will twitch, it will take another step forward, its tail goes up, and it's away, full of confidence. The Vizsla usually behaves in this manner, rather than barging forward.

So we see our little Vizsla's personality developing: its active brain is responsive to all new stimuli, to being moulded and formed in the most receptive way. When a novice puppy owner asks the question "When shall I start training?" He may have something specific in mind. But in fact, the groundwork is already in progress, and has been from birth. Essentially, the puppy has learned to relate to humans, it wishes to please, and it wants to be with you. Are you both ready for the next stage of your education?

OBJECTIVES

What is your ambition for your Vizsla? Are you the sort of owner who muddles along from day to day, issuing ineffective commands to your puppy? Are you the person who promises

A typical Vizsla's reaction to a new situation: inquisitive, but hesitating. O'Connell.

The puppy cannot resist investigating...   *O'Connell.*

In no time the puppy stands its ground, full of confidence.   *O'Connell.*

to train, but always tomorrow? Or have you decided on a goal? Do you wish to use your Vizsla as a gundog? Do you intend to train it to the stage where it could compete in working tests or field trials; or to beat or pick up on your local rough shoot? Or you may choose to specialise in Agility, Obedience, Falconry or Deer Stalking. However, for those with less ambition, the aim is to have a well trained dog, and this can be a joy in itself. What could be more fulfilling than to walk with your well-mannered Vizsla companion, so well controlled it may run ahead, without chasing or running amok. Then, with a call "Come" or "Heel", it returns to you, and at the command "Sit", it sits by you until you continue on. How has this happy partnership been achieved? The answer is by learning and training together.

There are excellent text books written by professional gundog trainers, and there are many training groups for the HPRs with excellent facilities, and trainers who welcome novice handlers. If you have never trained a Vizsla before, it can be intimidating to take on the task ahead, made even more so by the 'instant expert', who would like everyone to believe that only he has the answer. The dyed-in-the-wool gundog trainers are rarely unwilling to help a beginner, and it is expert advice and help you will need. Above all, watch the Vizslas working. You will see then that all of us make mistakes; and we have all made mistakes we have come to regret. When you are ready, take your Vizsla to classes, but meanwhile, there is much you can prepare it for.

One of the initial failings in dog training is that it has not been appreciated that the whole subject of learning starts as soon as the puppy is able to respond to you. The following sections on 'Play Training' and 'Early Training' are intended as a guide to answer some of the questions a novice asks when anticipating training his Vizsla gundog – and to encourage sensible owners to have a go.

FIRST STAGE

PLAY TRAINING

Much of a puppy's early play-learning evolves as the result of the owner's actions, rather than being consciously taught as a lesson. The puppy learns quietly without stress or any real effort, but it is invaluable as part of its upbringing. For instance, a whole litter of puppies learns to "Come", as a reflex to the breeder's call "Come", softly clapping his hands and walking backwards, encouraging the puppies to follow. The team does so, tumbling and tripping as fast as they can to get to him. All sorts of little lessons can be taught. The puppies will follow the breeder if he walks forward, patting his left thigh softly. He calls "Heel" in a playful voice, and the troupe will be happy to follow.

When you have your puppy home with you, if you know the breeder's pattern of behaviour with the puppy, you will find the puppy automatically responds. If you use the word "Come", already familiar, as he is coming towards you, clap your hands softly, or pat your knee, and the puppy soon learns that it will receive a warm cuddle from you. You can teach your puppy to sit by you, if you kneel down holding it to your side firmly, with your right hand on its chest and the left gently pushing its rear down to sit, and saying "Sit". When the puppy sits, stroke its back and chest soothingly, and give plenty of praise. The most convenient word, "No", can be learnt by your puppy long before it is old enough to take formal lessons in obedience. Use the command "No" in a gruff voice, removing the puppy from whatever it is that is forbidden. At first, of course, it will not understand, but by repeating the word and the action, it will get the message. You will soon discover how responsive a puppy of this age can be. When it has done the right thing, reward it in a light, joyful tone of voice, so that it knows it has pleased you. A puppy will learn to go to its basket, if you use the same word each time the pup climbs into its basket. It will not be long before you can give the command "Basket", and the puppy will know what you mean. By now, the puppy has learnt its name, and it is beginning to know that when you command, if it responds, you automatically praise; thus it is learning 'responsive reflex'.

SECOND STAGE

EARLY TRAINING

One of the arts of a good trainer is to assess the temperament and trainability of his Vizsla. Only you, the owner, will learn to know how ready your puppy is to go on to the Early Training stage, and at what pace to develop its training. A puppy learns extremely quickly, so it is easy for you to advance too quickly, putting pressure on the pup unknowingly, and causing behavioural problems that are difficult to deal with. Stubbornness, loss of drive and enthusiasm for work, are signs of too much too soon. This does not mean to say that the minute it is playtime, the puppy will not be back to its old self. Anticipate and recognise sulky symptoms, and correct your mistake by doing a simple exercise that you both know and do well, and always finish on a good note.

The balance is a tricky one. Novice trainers often skimp essential early obedience training, and fail to gain any sort of control before going on to the next stage. On the other hand, it is equally wrong to overdo the disciplining, with endless domination, endless sitting, staying and heeling; if you are getting bored, you can be sure that your Viszla is. So keep the lessons short and interesting, and change the location. You can do a lot of early work in the house or garden or in the yard, as a puppy will be distracted at this stage in open places. It cannot be expected to concentrate for long: little and often is the key.

What can we expect our puppy to have learned by the time it is six months old?

1. To walk to heel, on and off the lead.
2. To sit.
3. To stay.
4. To come.

TO HEEL

THE AIM: The aim of this exercise is to get your dog walking calmly on your left-handside off the lead, on the command "Heel". We are not asking for the leg-hugging, eyes-on-you, 'obedience' trained dog, but a controlled dog, with an outward-looking aspect. Your attitude is that your Vizsla is by now perfectly capable of performing this task; your manner is firm and businesslike, and you are generous in your praise.

THE METHOD: Walk briskly with your dog on your left, on the lead. The end of the lead should be in your right hand, and your left hand should be halfway down the lead. Keep the dog's attention by talking to it. As it walks forward and the lead tightens, give the command "Heel", with a short, sharp tug to bring the dog level to your knee. Immediately slacken the lead, praise the dog, and walk on briskly, patting your thigh to encourage the dog to walk with you. Repeat this until it has got the message. The immediate slackening of the lead and your praise is the reward. If the dog gets distracted say "No", and walk on smartly. If the dog persists in pulling, if your tug is not sharp enough, and it is not heeling your command, try using a deeper voice. To keep the dog interested, give it surprises, walk in a circle, or to the right or left, change your pace from fast to slow; this helps the dog to concentrate, because it does not know what you are going to do next. When the dog has learned this lesson on the lead, it can do the same exercise off the lead. If the dog starts to wander, call it sharply, pat your thigh, and run forward a few steps to encourage it to follow.

SIT AND STAY

THE AIM: The aim of this lesson is for your Vizsla to sit by your side off the lead, on command, and to walk forward with you on the command "Heel", or to remain sitting on the word "Stay", as you walk on. This is the very basis of steadiness that the gundog has to adhere to, and it should become second nature, whether at a distance or close to. It is this training that ultimately makes the dog steady in the field. All its instincts are to run and chase. The most important lesson of all is for the dog to sit when something runs or falls, and this is most difficult, because it goes against all that the dog wants to do.

THE METHOD: With your Vizsla on the lead, walk briskly forward with the dog at heel, and holding the lead in your right hand. Then give the command "Sit", tightening the lead to pull the dog's head up, simultaneously putting your left hand on its rump, to push its quarters down. When the dog sits, allow the lead to loop loosely and stroke its back. Hold this position for a few moments, then strike off with your left foot, tightening the lead up and walk on with the dog at heel. When it is able to obey this command at any time you wish, you can combine heeling off the lead with sitting off the lead.

When you have mastered this, you can move on to the first distance control by teaching your Vizsla to stay. Start by walking your dog to heel on the lead, then command the dog to sit, and allow the lead to lie in front of it. Step forward in front of your dog, raise your right hand, palm open, turned toward the dog, and command "Stay". If the dog moves, say "No", and put it gently back in position. Be firm and repeat the exercise. Once the dog is settled, take a step or two back with your hand up saying "Stay". Wait and return to the dog calmly, stand by its side, pick up the lead, and pause, making sure it does not move until you end the lesson. Praise the dog and let it run about to stretch its legs, and to give you both a break.

The day you feel your dog is confident and steady, you can repeat this without the lead. You can walk a few more paces back, or you may walk round the dog in an ever-widening circle. At this stage never go out of sight; always go back to the dog. This exercise is for building trust as well; the dog learns that even if you go away, you will always come back. Do nothing to make the dog feel insecure. Why do we use the word 'Stay', when it would seem simpler to use 'Sit'? Your dog walks to heel, you stop, it sits; you walk on and it follows. 'Stay' means it remains sitting while you walk on.

<u>Reminder</u> Command, response, praise. If at any time your dog is not being responsive, go back to a lesson it can do, and end on a good note, so that you can praise. Always have the lead loose if your dog has responded correctly; it should only be tightened on a command, which should be short, sharp and effective. Loose lead is the reward, tight lead is the correction. A mistake that is easily made is to train your dog to heel on the left, but if it is to work with a handler or shooter who is left-handed, it must be taught to heel on the right.

THE RECALL – TO COME

Your Vizsla needs to learn to come to you on the command "Come", at all times, so that it is entirely under your control when it is off the lead.

THE METHOD: Your dog will be familiar with the word "Come", but our wayward Vizsla will go 'deaf' at times, and now the lesson needs to be reinforced. You want your Vizsla to love running to you; so, at this stage, you can bend down with your arms wide open to receive the dog. Let it know that you are overwhelmed by affection and its cleverness when it arrives. If it hesitates, walk a few steps back. Do not curb its enthusiastic rush toward you. Do not call from the 'Sit' – it can make the dog unsteady – call the dog when it is moving toward you. Repeat this command on all occasions when you want the dog: calling it for a walk, for its food, or when you want to give the dog a cuddle, so that the word becomes second nature.

Never chase your dog, always get it to come to you. If there are times when it is reluctant to listen, go away from the dog, and it will follow. Never punish the dog when it arrives, or it will be unwilling to come to you. If it is not responding to you, go back to basics: call the dog when it is near to you, praise, and repeat.

TO SEEK ON

One of the biggest mistakes we can make with this breed is to get our Vizsla to a high standard of obedience and steadiness, only to find that it is so wanting to please us, it does not want to leave our side. Comes the time we want it to hunt out; we find that it has no wish to. The dog is too uncertain of itself; all drive and enthusiasm are gone. It is so inhibited that it has become a potterer. It is so drummed into handlers that the gundog must be steady and must obey, that we ourselves become inhibited, not daring to let our Vizslas run free. The dog becomes so reliant on its handler for orders, it never stops looking up for the next command.

THE AIM: So how can we make sure that this does not happen? This is where your skill at reading your dog comes into play. Besides giving lessons in manners, you must also give your dog all the encouragement you can to help it have a sense of independence and allow its instincts to mature. This character building and boosting of self-esteem runs parallel with its formal training at a different time and place. Wherever you take your young puppy, let it delight in discovering things for itself. When it shows enthusiasm and keen interest in searching out hedges, ditches and clumps of long grass, imbue the dog with your enthusiasm. Encourage it to "Seek On" or "Get On", as it is questing ahead. Let the dog work out a patch of cover; give it free rein, give it your permission to hunt. When the dog catches a scent on the light breeze, stay quiet, let it find out where it comes from. If the dog goes out too far for comfort, call it back or check it, then wave it on. The dog is learning to use its inborn instinct; it becomes stimulated to want more, so urge the dog on. It will soon learn that "Seek On" means 'There might be something interesting, I had better go and have a look'. These are the early beginnings of your dog working for you in the field. Of course, there is a fine balance between pleasing you and pleasing itself, and at all times the scales must be tipped toward you. The dog must know that it has to have your permission to do what it wants. This strengthens your closer rapport, mutual respect and trust. More than anything, let the dog enjoy itself and have fun. Let it feel free.

WORDS OF COMMAND, HAND SIGNALS AND WHISTLE

You have been using words of command and hand signals initially. Now you need to use the whistle as well. This will be essential to use when the dog is at any distance – far easier to use a few well chosen pips on the whistle than using your voice. It is also less stirring for game than the human voice. There are bound to be times when your Vizsla can neither see you nor hear your voice, but the pitch of the whistle cannot be ignored. When you have decided which words and whistle commands you are going to use – and I realise that handlers will use different terms, e.g. "Hup" for sit – you must always stick to them, using your dog's name at all times. For example: "Rex, sit", whistle and hand signal.

The handler demonstrates arm signals with Szajani Brokat, aged nine months. Bred, owned and handled by S. Harris.   *Pictures: S. Hart.*

'Sit'

'Come'

Arm right – to go right.

'Get back'

ACTION	**VOICE**	**WHISTLE**	**SIGNAL**
To walk on heel	"Heel"		Pat thigh.
To sit	"Sit"	Long blast	Raised hand, palm outward.
To stay	"Stay"	Long blast	Raised hand, palm outward.
To come	"Come"	Three short blasts	Pat knee or open arms.
To quest ahead	"Get on", "Seek on"		Under arm wave forward.
To retrieve	"Fetch"		Arm outstretched in direction, or wave of hand.
Look up for signal		Two short blasts	
To range out left	"Get out"		Left arm to the left.
To range right	"Get out"		Right arm to the right.
Get back	"Get back"		Raise arm as if pushing door.
At point or area of retrieve	"Hie lost"		
To deliver retrieve	"Give", "Dead"		Reach out with hand.
To jump	"Over"		Point to obstacle.
Enter cover or water	"Get in"		Point to cover or water.
To watch the fall of object	"Mark"		

Some breeds are taught commands of obedience using the food bowl as a reward. For example: "Rex, Sit", putting the bowl down and making the dog wait. This may not suit your Vizsla; it can cause upset. Any association with food as a form of punishment or reward may confuse the dog. Its reward is your affection, which it thrives on.

LESSON FOR TRAINER

1. Give clear, precise, simple, commands.
2. Command, response, praise.
3. Normal voice for command, deep voice for disapproval, light voice for praise.
4. If you are tense, irritable or angry, never attempt to teach your dog that day.
5. A lesson may seem ragged in performance one day, but the following, when both of you come to it fresh, the dog may perform with excellence.
6. We have gone through the lessons that are fundamental for your dog. If you are teaching your Vizsla a new exercise, start with one it knows: walking to heel or sit and stay. This will help to get the dog in the right frame of mind – and you as well, for that matter.

Chapter Ten

RETRIEVES

THIRD STAGE

ADVANCED TRAINING

If your Vizsla is to retrieve tenderly – and the majority of Vizslas are tender-mouthed – it is essential that nothing is done to make the dog hard-mouthed. Rough games of tug-of-war, or pulling objects away from the dog, will teach it to grip hard so that there will be teeth marks, so hard that when the dog comes to dummy work, and ultimately to pick up a bird, it will crunch it – the ultimate crime! Puppies frequently pick up objects to carry about. It may be a nuisance, but do not be tempted to scold the pup; it is a natural instinct to retrieve, so receive the 'present' graciously, take it gently, using the word "Give" or "Dead". You are on the way to its picking a dummy tenderly, and to bringing a 'Bird to Hand', which the Vizsla must do if it is to be your gundog.

Accepting that set rules are not infallible for training, it does no harm to have expectations and guidelines. When you are training your Vizsla it is essential to react as the situation demands. It is better to avoid confrontation, if there is a way round it; it is better to be flexible. In some instances, our timing can often set up a pattern of resistance, so sometimes it is advisable to put off what your Vizsla will not or cannot do today, until tomorrow. It goes against the grain, but it works, and that is what you want.

You can anticipate that your Vizsla may be able to cope with the following exercises by the time it is a year old:

1. The retrieve and steadiness. 2. The drop.
3. Water. 4. The shot.

RETRIEVING AND STEADINESS

The Vizsla should be a natural retriever, and it is so tempting when your puppy brings you objects, such as sticks and balls, to throw them for the dog to retrieve. However, you must resist the temptation, or the dog will make it an obsessional game, which is fatal, if you want a gundog. The dummy, and ultimately game, must be seen as belonging to the dog's master, not to the dog. The dog is allowed to retrieve as a favour to you, and so it learns to work for you.

If your puppy sits by you as young as seven weeks old, you can roll out an object such as a carrot, which is a good shape for carrying. Let the puppy run out to collect the carrot, and when it returns to you, give plenty of praise. Let the pup walk holding the carrot for a little, so that it enjoys the experience and feels your pleasure. Then gently take the carrot from the pup, saying "Give" or "Dead". Do not be tempted to repeat this more than a couple of times, and never leave the 'treasure' for the puppy to chew. Keep it as a treat. A pheasant wing can be another useful retrieve for your puppy.

THE AIM: Your aim is to teach your Vizsla to retrieve a dummy on command, so that ultimately it will retrieve shot game to hand. The dog must first learn to fetch the dummy, using its eyes to mark the fall and its nose to find the object. The dog has to learn to sit without moving until it is told to fetch. It must also learn to retrieve from water. Later on the dog has to make the transition from dummies to the real thing.

If you are fortunate enough to have a companion 'dummy thrower', it will make your job easier, but there are many occasions when you and your Vizsla are on your own, and I prefer training in this situation because it is less formal. I do not feel pressurized, and therefore the Vizslas are relaxed. I incorporate much of my training on walks, either where there is game, or where there is some temptation of scent of rabbits. Thus they learn to use their noses and develop their game-finding abilities at their own pace. But ultimately, you need to do your basic dummy retrieves where there are no distractions. If a dog has no temptation, you will never know whether your methods are working or not. As I prefer to train on my own, I have described the retrieves from this viewpoint. However, many prefer to work in a different manner, and enlist the help of a partner for retrieve work. The style of working does not matter, as long as the Vizsla is working for you.

There are three types of progressive basic retrieves: "the seen", "memory" and "blind".

THE SEEN RETRIEVE

The weight of the dummy you choose should be light enough for your puppy to pick up, but not so light that the pup is tempted to play with it, nor should it be too heavy, so that the

Reach forward and take the dummy on the command. Russetmantle Mist, owned and handled by S. Mildwinsky. Bred by G. Gottlieb.   *P. Gliddon.*

puppy finds it an effort to lift. A one-pounder should suit most puppies to begin with. You may use a heavier one as the puppy grows on. Always use the words "Hie Lost" as the pup gets into the area of the retrieve; this tells the puppy that it is in the location. To start your puppy off, try an initial retrieve informally. Choose a passageway or hall where the puppy cannot run past you. Throw the dummy out where it can be seen, and just let the puppy run and pick it up. The puppy may pounce on it, or drag it from one end to begin with. Never mind, let the puppy get the feel of the dummy. The object is for the pup to run forward, pick up the dummy and carry it, however imperfectly. Once you know your puppy will retrieve in this way, give it one or two more throws, and that's enough. At this stage kneel down when the pup is running back to you, welcoming it with your arms wide open. Remember: command, response and praise!

Sooner or later you will need to find a quiet place outside – a narrow lane, track or pathway. Repeat the same retrieve, throwing the dummy as before, with the command "Fetch", as the puppy goes out. When the pup runs back, welcome it into your arms; let it strut round a bit and then gently take the dummy from its mouth. If the puppy is happy, and does not seem reluctant to pick up the object, the next step is to restrain the pup with your hand on its chest, only letting go on the word "Fetch"; this time encourage the puppy to retrieve to hand. You can then move on, with the puppy sitting, and throw the dummy into a clump of grass, so that it sees the fall and 'marks' it. In this way it learns to 'mark' the fall and to use its nose for scenting it.

If your Vizsla is hesitant to pick up the dummy at first, tempt it by pushing or rolling the dummy about, and enticing it to pick it up. If your puppy starts to mess about with the dummy, either when it is picking it up, or coming back with it to you, never go towards the puppy, always go away. To begin with, try backing off a few steps to encourage the puppy to follow, or if it does not respond, try running away. When the puppy does arrive, do not chastise it, or it will hesitate to come in when it has been misbehaving. Some trainers like the dog to sit in front of them with the dummy on return. This is yet more discipline, especially at this stage. However, the puppy must not drop the retrieve; you must reach forward and take from the puppy on command.

If your Vizsla tends to drop the dummy at your feet, place your hands gently round the dog's muzzle with the dummy in its mouth and command "Hold". Praise the dog immediately on releasing your hands; then command "Give" or "Dead". Encourage the dog to "Hold" while it is walking about with the dummy until you command it to "Give". Make sure you give clear instructions: "Hold" and praise; "Give" and praise. If you are too aggressive with your commands, watch that the dog does not mark the dummy with its teeth out of anxiety.

THE MEMORY RETRIEVE

Your Vizsla may not be too happy on a seen retrieve. It may find the memory retrieve much more interesting; it will have to concentrate and work harder for it.

METHOD: Walk forward with your Vizsla at your heel. Make it sit, and throw the dummy ahead, making sure the dog marks it. Then turn away with the dog, commanding "Heel", firmly. The dog will show some resistance, because it will want to go straight to the dummy. If the dog does not obey, you can slip on its lead. Then walk a fair distance, put the dog in the sit, and give the command "Fetch", and urge the dog to go straight to the dummy.

THE BLIND RETRIEVE

Give your Vizsla a memory retrieve to start with, then put the dummy in exactly the same spot, without letting the dog mark it. Walk away with the dog, and then send it back to fetch the dummy, just as you did before. By doing the memory retrieve first, the dog will instinctively return to that spot. This exercise teaches your Vizsla to trust you, and it learns that "Fetch" means that there is something to retrieve, even though it has not seen it being thrown.

CONCLUSION: These three retrieves teach your Vizsla to go straight to the dummy, and ultimately to dead game, on the command "Fetch". The dog knows that when you give this command, there is something to retrieve.

GET BACK AND FETCH

THE AIM: When your Vizsla has mastered the seen, memory and blind retrieves, sooner or later the command "Get back and fetch" must be incorporated. This exercise is invaluable if the dog cannot locate the dummy or shot game. It is a directional command for the dog to go back in a straight line to find the object.

THE METHOD: With your Vizsla sitting at heel, throw the dummy into a clump of grass. Walk away with the dog at heel for about twelve yards. Put the dog in the sit, and stand in front, backing away several paces and commanding it to "Get back and fetch". Use the hand signal as if pushing open a heavy door. If the dog does not understand at first, go back a little way with it, and encourage it to fetch the dummy. When the dog has learnt this exercise, you can drop the dummy without it knowing. Eventually, when you feel the dog is ready and can be trusted, widen the distance between the dog and the dummy, and between you and the dog. For some reason dogs seem to love this lesson, and when you walk away, most dogs cannot wait to fly off to find the dummy – so make sure your Vizsla is rock steady before you attempt to widen the distance. Make sure your Vizsla is working into the wind (wind coming towards you), so that the scent of the dummy is wafting towards the dog. This helps to develop its instinctive power of scenting.

It is very important for your Vizsla to acknowledge that not every retrieve is for it. There will be many times out shooting when a bird shot will not necessarily be for your dog to retrieve, but for another dog on the shoot, or birds may be falling all around, but it must not

*Four steady
Vizslas mark the
fall of the
dummies.*
                    S. Hart.

budge until the end of the drive. So in your lessons, it is a good idea for you to collect the dummy sometimes. A useful exercise is to sit the dog at a distance and lob four or five dummies all around it – behind, in front and on either side; as each falls, command "Sit", with the appropriate hand signal. Do not hurl the dummies at the dog or frighten it. If the dog seems scared, just throw one or two dummies about when it is by you, until it gets used to the exercise. If the dog gets up from its sitting position at a distance, return it to exactly the same spot (if a dog ever moves off from the sit, always put it back to the same place, and never let it creep forward). Make the dog sit while you pick up each dummy, making sure the dog remains in its place. Then go to the dog, and give plenty of praise. Another useful exercise is to walk the dog at heel past the dummies. If it goes toward one, give the command "No" or "Leave" and walk on smartly. When you have walked past all the dummies put the dog in the 'sit' while you go back to pick them up. A youngster can become so excited by retrieving game that it may attempt to grab a bird from another dog's mouth – a dreadful crime, out shooting. The command "No" or "Leave" will act as a reminder.

The split retrieve: Bend down to help your dog locate the second dummy by signalling with your arm to direct its gaze.
Russetmantle Leasal.   Owner/handler L. Wilks.   *Ryan.*

THE SPLIT RETRIEVE AND DROP

By now your youngster should be steady to thrown dummies, but if you are not confident, go back to earlier exercises. It is better to reinforce training, rather than progress to more advanced lessons, for the moment.

THE AIM: The following exercises will increase your ability to direct and redirect your Vizsla close to, or at a distance, so that it can get into the area of the fall of the dummy. You may also teach the dog to "Drop", i.e. sit the dog at a distance in order to stop it, or to redirect it. This is an extension of all that you have already taught your dog in steadiness, at a distance. It is essential for its work in the field when the dog must never run in, or chase. If you can command "Sit" in any situation where the dog may be tempted, and it responds, it is a great achievement.

THE METHOD: It is essential that your dog distinguishes left and right hand commands. This is achieved by sitting your dog with its back to a wall, hedge or fence. Throw a dummy to its right, on the command "Fetch", and positive arm direction to the right, cast the dog out; on its return to you, put the dog back in the same spot, and repeat the exercise to the left. Another type of retrieve for concentration and steadiness is to have your Vizsla sitting at heel, and a dummy is thrown far out to the right, and one to the left, and the dog must mark both. You can command "Mark" as each one is thrown. The dog will want to retrieve the last dummy thrown. Send the dog to collect the dummy, using appropriate arm signals. On its return, take this dummy and bend down to help the dog locate the second dummy by signalling with your arm to direct its gaze, and saying "Mark". Send the dog to fetch the dummy, remembering in all retrieves that "Hie Lost" tells the dog that it is in the right location. Once the dog can perform this exercise, you may direct it on to whichever dummy you wish. Remember to correct by saying "No", if the dog goes for the wrong dummy. You can introduce the 'Drop' at this stage. Sit the dog at a distance and redirect it to the correct dummy.

Having mastered this retrieve, the dog can be given one seen and one unseen retrieve. Always make sure it has to work to find the dummies – all these variations will keep it on its toes. It can also be given different types of dummies, such as wrapping a rabbit skin round one and pheasant feathers round another.

By now your Vizsla will have had a wide experience: its steadiness is becoming second nature, its concentration will have improved and it will have learned to persevere.

INTRODUCING YOUR VIZSLA TO THE REAL THING

My puppies are brought up with the scent of game: domestic chickens, geese, swans, moorhens and duck. If a dog wants to nose the dead game or drag a dead rabbit a little way, they may, but it must not be used to shake as a plaything. At some time during your programme you can introduce your Vizsla to the real thing: a dead rabbit, pigeon, pheasant or partridge. Initially it must be cold game. If the dog is used to the rabbit skin and pheasant dummy, it will be accustomed to the feel in its mouth. Let the dog smell and nuzzle the game while you carry it. The dog will be curious, so give it time to nose the object. Once the scent is familiar, give the dog a simple retrieve out of sight, with the command "Fetch". The dog may take time to turn the game over and work out how to lift it, putting it down to re-position this unfamiliar thing until it has a firm, but gentle hold. Let the dog strut around with the game, do not take it away at first. If the dog has no problem with cold game, after a time you can introduce it to warm game.

If your dog refuses to pick up a pigeon, it may be because the feathers are too soft and loose, and the dog finds this unpleasant in its mouth. For those who feel there may be a problem, try putting a pigeon in an old sock or a pheasant in a sock with the foot cut at the end. Sometimes a dog will retrieve more eagerly from water to begin with.

Some dogs have no problem in picking up game, others find the transition difficult. As in all aspects of training, no two dogs are alike in response to retrieving. One youngster could be taken out with a gun and pick up anything that is shot, whereas another could take up to two years of gentle progressive training before being persuaded to pick up or carry a warm bird. Others may refuse to pick up dummies, but are quite happy picking up game. However, generally speaking, Vizslas are regarded as effiicient and reliable retrievers.

It does not take the Vizsla long to get used to water: Ch. Russetmantle Troy and grandson Ch. Russetmantle Quiver.   *S. Gottlieb.*

THE WATER RETRIEVE

Introduce your Vizsla puppy to water so that it grows up enjoying a swim. The Vizsla is a powerful and agile swimmer. There should be no reason why it should not take to this experience like the proverbial duck. A dog should never be pushed or thrown into water; urge it and invite it to have a happy time, and it will respond.

THE AIM: Your Vizsla must be prepared to retrieve from water at any distance, or to swim across any stretch to retrieve a dummy or game from the far bank and the land beyond, either on a seen or a blind retrieve. The dog must learn to hunt the bank on your instructions and commands. Remember it must not be a self-hunter.

METHOD: Your puppy can be taken paddling as soon as you both feel like It. Choose a warm day, and let the pup play about in the shallows. Gentle play and splashing about with other dogs will give the puppy confidence. Sooner or later it will find itself swimming with its elders. Thus swimming becomes second nature, as will retrieving in water. Start by throwing a dummy into the shallows, and the dog will come strutting out with it. Do not take the dummy away to begin with; let the dog enjoy every minute of its triumph.

When you are both ready for more formal training, take your Vizsla out on its own, and

Soon swimming will become second nature, as will retrieving from water. C. Paul.

Russetmantle Fennel completes a water retrieve. D. Ryan.

Russetmantle Flake waits for the command to retrieve across water.

give it seen retrieves in water, not too far at first, and then further and further out, until the dog is responding to commands and signals as it would on land. At a more advanced stage you will want the dog to learn to retrieve from the opposite bank. This lesson is not difficult if is it taught across a river that is not too wide, nor with a strong current. Beware if you use a pond: a Vizsla is not stupid, and it will try to run round on land on its return!

A BLIND RETRIEVE ACROSS WATER

THE AIM To get your dog into the water on the command "Get In", across the water commanding "Get On", and up the bank commanding "Get Out" – or whatever commands you wish to use.

METHOD Give your Vizsla a seen, marked retrieve on the far bank. Once it gets to know there is something exciting happening over there, give an unseen retrieve. This progression is similar to the memory retrieve exercise, leading to the blind retrieve on land. So, put the dog sitting where it cannot see you (remember to tell it to stay). Return to the bank, throw the dummy over to the opposite side, allowing your Vizsla to hear the fall, but not to mark it. Bring the dog back and indicate where the dummy is, and then send the dog across. If you throw the dummy in the same area as before, this lesson tells the dog that even if it does not see the fall, if you give the command to get over, there is something to retrieve.

Your Vizsla can learn to jump obstacles. Waidman Lulu, owned and bred by L. Petrie Hay.

Finally, the most advanced lesson. Give the dog an unseen, unheard retrieve, well beyond the bank (someone else will have to put the dummy in place for you). The dog may have to hunt, and so it must take directions from you if it has difficulty locating its retrieve. Always work your dog into the wind on these retrieves if you can.

CONCLUSION: These retrieves will really stretch your Vizsla, but it can be great fun, if you make it so. One day you will find you cannot keep your dog out of the water. However, if your Vizsla is sticky about water and obviously is not too keen, wade in with the dog, or have a swim as well, when you are introducing it to water for the first time. If it still fails to respond, leave it until the dog feels braver.

All dogs want to shake when they come out of the water, but if you allow your Vizsla to get into this habit, it will drop the retrieve. To prevent this happening, reach out to take the retrieve as soon as you can, or try backing off, giving the impression that you may be going. The dog will then want to follow after you, and will be more concerned with retrieving to you than shaking or dropping the dummy. As long as the dog holds the dummy, it is allowed to shake.

Never give your Vizsla too many retrieves, however much it enjoys them. The dog will get bored, and then you will get yourself into the confrontation syndrome. Always get the dog to come to you, never go to the dog. At this advanced stage it still needs praise every time it completes an exercise correctly. You will be proud of your Vizsla when he retrieves a big fat Mallard!

Your Vizsla can also learn to jump obstacles, and it will have fun leaping over logs, a low fence, bales of straw, and eventually a gate. Use the word "Hup", so that when the dog comes out shooting and may need to pick up a bird that has landed on the other side of a fence, your command "Hup" will send it over. The dog will then retrieve the bird and jump back over in style, bringing the bird to hand.

Chapter Eleven

HUNTING AND POINTING

STEADY TO SHOT AND THE DROP

THE AIM To get your Vizsla so accustomed to the sound of shot, it can work for the shooter happily; to train the dog to respond to the sound of shot instantly, as it would on your command "Sit".

METHOD A puppy should be accustomed to all manner of loud noises – banging doors, pots and pans clanging, you clapping your hands suddenly and loudly. The dog may also be used to gunfire and bird-scarers at a distance. But there is nothing so thunderingly loud as the real thing, close to; so it is essential to introduce a dog to gunfire carefully, and with caution, or it will become gun-shy, or at least noise-nervous. However careful you are, many handlers find their dogs may take a shooting season before they are entirely settled. Do not make a fuss, just keep your dog near you if it seems intimidated or cowed. Once it feels secure, it will learn that the noise means excitement, and it will not be hurt. Do not fuss over the dog, or it will respond to your concern, which will make matters worse. A gun-shy dog either takes off to the next county, digs a hole or clings to its handler like a limpet.

Allow your dog to become accustomed to the sight of a gun: hold it high and swing it down. Have a friendly shooter fire some shots for you a good distance away. If all is well and your Vizsla is hunting about happily, walk closer, and so on. Do not be tempted to go too near at first. Once it is accustomed to the noise, whenever the gun is fired and wherever the dog is, make it sit: this conditions it to 'Drop to Shot'.

You may also introduce the shot and fall of the dummy; a dummy launcher is useful here.

Do not let the dog retrieve the dummy at first, and when you do, only let it retrieve one every now and then; you must retrieve the dummy yourself, or allow another dog to get it. This teaches your dog two things:

1. The shot is not a signal to 'retrieve', it is a signal to 'drop'.
2. A retrieve is only for the dog sent out for it.

   In the field, out shooting, there is no worse crime than running in on another dog's retrieve, or for that matter, 'running in'. This is the time when you, and the rapport that you have with your Vizsla, is really tested. When you work your dog in the field, the temptations for the dog are enormous; it is so exciting. If a dog does start to 'run in', you have to be down on it like a ton of bricks, because it means the dog is not listening to you, it is responding to its instinct to chase.

   By now, trust and confidence should be mutual, and you should know to what degree you can admonish your Vizsla. If it has flouted your authority, it must be dealt with in no uncertain terms. If you are too frightened of upsetting the dog, and it cannot accept your displeasure, either you are being too harsh and your training has slipped up somewhere, or the dog is folding because you have not instilled confidence, so your anger shatters its self-esteem. The answer is to go back to the drawing-board.

CONCLUSION

Whatever you are doing with your Vizsla, however near or far it is from you, it must 'drop' on your command – that is to say on the command "Sit", either using voice, signal or whistle. The dog must be so conditioned by now that it is an entirely automatic reflex to sit. It may be out of sight: you blow your whistle – and the dog must drop. It may be about to run across a busy road, a rabbit shoots past under its nose, a bird is shot, it is down and runs, it wants to chase it – but if you blow your whistle, the dog 'drops'. Your reaction has to be quicker than the dog's; anticipation is your key. It is vital that you never give the command to drop when the dog is coming to you, until it is fully trained, or it will start to slow up, anticipating that you are going to give the command to stop, and it will start to creep towards you. If there is no alternative and you have to command "Drop" on the way back, try not repeat it.

HUNTING AND POINTING

Before we continue I cannot emphasise enough that from the earliest opportunity your Vizsla puppy should run freely; always let it explore the delights of a hedgerow and the joys of hunting, so that its natural inborn instincts develop alongside its formal training . This is the period when the puppy learns from its own initiative, with you as a companion; a time when it discovers the elusive myriad of scents, and its concentration sharpens its nose.

Szajani Aniko has been trialled successfully for the last few seasons. In 1991-92 she gained many awards in the field, handled by her owner Sue Farquar. Bred by S. Harris

When the dog learns sensibility, its acute sensitivity heightens and comes into its own: it hears every stick that snaps, every wild animal that moves, it scents the minutest puff of wind, its eyes watch and wait, it acquires field-nous of its own. Obviously, if your dog is a hard-headed, obstinate, fearless youngster, an extrovert and a natural keen hunter, you will need to dampen its enthusiasm at times; if it takes liberties, you can always check it. But a naturally quiet, solemn, more introverted Vizsla needs urging on. If you need to stir up a bit of keenness, allow the dog a chase or two, but only when you permit it.

While you are training your Vizsla on retrieves, it can progress at the same time with hunting and pointing, but this must be kept separate from its retrieving schedule. So take the dog to a different location. Eventually the three elements, hunting, pointing and retrieving will be performed together, but not until the dog is ready. When your dog starts to accompany you out shooting great care has to be taken that its game-finding and retrieving are kept separate, until you have confidence that it will not 'run in'.

QUARTERING

A Vizsla is every bit as capable of working out with drive as any of the HPRs; it has an excellent nose and hunts at pace. It can search keenly and systematically every area of ground, keeping within reasonable distance of its handler, leaving no game undetected.

Up until now you have given and encouraged your Vizsla to have free range. You have fostered the dog's abilities to hunt and recognise scent of game and to acknowledge it. As you are encouraging the dog to run freely, you may find that it quite naturally changes direction, as you do. Allow the puppy to range across you to the other side, and change your direction again when you think it has gone far enough. In this way it is learning to quarter quite naturally. This may become second nature – to work at speed into the wind, using its nose to scent, before you introduce any discipline. Do not clutter the dog with shouts and whistles or directions – put your hands in your pockets!

Scent is a major factor in hunting. Whatever direction the wind is coming from, the dog has to work into it, facing the on-coming breeze, so that scent comes towards it. In most conditions your Vizsla will work on air-born scent, with its head up, as opposed to ground-scenting with nose down. It is exciting to see a youngster learn to turn its head into the wind to catch an on-coming scent. Some have keener noses than others. A novice dog may tend to keep its nose on the ground; in this situation attract its attention and urge the dog on. The term used for systematic hunting and ground coverage to locate game is quartering. Your young Vizsla is now ready to be instructed in this exciting new element.

THE AIM To control the free-ranging instinct that the dog has acquired and foster its desire to hunt, so that it may learn to cover the ground efficiently, moving backwards and forwards into the wind. Eventually it must be capable of working in front of its handler or shooter or a line of guns on any given terrain, keeping ahead and within range, conscientiously searching for game to point.

METHOD Choose an open field of grass or stubble where the dog can hunt without the distraction of game about. Scent is generally good on a mild, warm, moist sort of day, when there is a light breeze. Do not take your Vizsla out on a very windy day to begin with; choose a day when the breeze is blowing toward you. Cast your Vizsla out to the left on command, giving a positive arm directive, walk purposefully to the left, urging it on if necessary. At about fifteen to twenty yards, pip on the whistle to turn, change direction and walk to the right and cast the dog out to the right. The reason for using your whistle is to get the dog to look at you, to see what you want it to do. As the dog becomes more experienced it learns to keep its attention on you, meaning that it is not self-hunting, and eventually you will not need to use the whistle. Remember, on the turn, the dog must go into the wind and travel diagonally across the face of the wind. Repeat this zigzag pattern until the dog's quartering becomes a rhythmical, methodical pattern, carried out at a steady pace. By now you can walk up in a straight line, while the dog covers the ground. (If at any time the dog comes on point, be prepared to let it point. You must put the bird up, and make your dog sit.)

If at any time the dog loses concentration, or goes out too far, you may call it in and start again, or give the command to drop, and cast the dog out again. Do not be tempted to let the dog range out too far at first or lengthen the beats, or it will get out of your control. Once the dog's quartering pattern is firmly established you can extend the limits, and when it is proficient enough, you may take him on to ground where there is game, providing the dog is steady enough and under control. But first, let us look at the principles of quartering and ground treatment in terms of using the wind.

ELEMENTARY PRINCIPLES IN SCENTING

UPWIND

Your Vizsla has learned that scent is brought on the on-coming breeze; it picks this scent up as it quarters across in front of you in such a pattern and distance and depth that it will not miss birds. When it has had sufficient experience, it will need to learn to use a side wind.

CHEEK WIND or SIDE WIND

There are times when the wind is not dead ahead, but coming from the side, blowing across the ground to be quartered. This means your Vizsla will need to pattern backwards and forwards moving directly from you for some eighty to a hundred yards, turn into the wind and work back towards you. It varies, of course; the wind may, more often than not, only be partially on the cheek. Consequently the dog has to slightly incline the angle of the pattern to capture as much of the wind as possible. You will find that it has to adapt its quartering so that it does not run behind you.

DOWN WIND

Your Vizsla needs to have acquired even more experience and game sense before it can be expected to handle a "Backwind" or "Down wind". The dog has to learn that it must run out at a distance of about eighty to a hundred yards, directed by the handler, and turn into the wind, taking the maximum advantage of the breeze coming towards it. All the ground ahead of you must be searched and covered by your Vizsla before you walk forward, otherwise you will put birds up yourself.

CASTING

The purpose of casting is to set your Vizsla out hunting into the wind, using the command "Seek On" or "Get On", with the appropriate arm signal. First of all you must assess the wind direction yourself; a novice can easily cast a dog out in the wrong direction. You need

Principles of wind

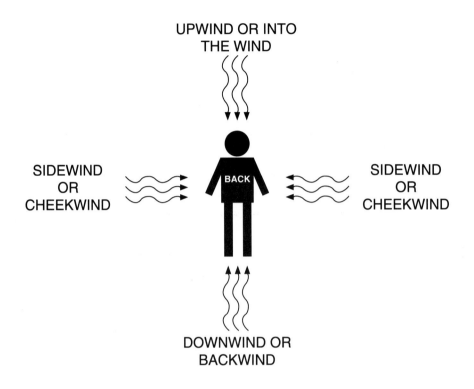

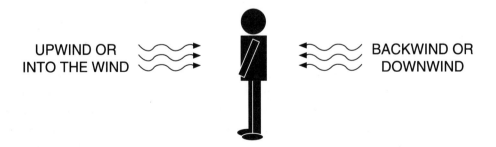

CHECK FROM WHICH DIRECTION THE WIND IS COMING

Casting

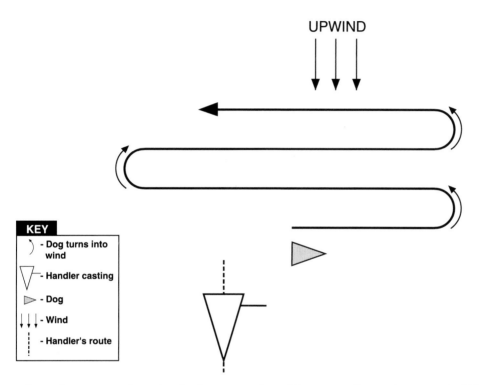

to learn how to regulate the dog's pace and position according to its natural ability. Do not impede the dog's natural instinct by lack of knowledge.

The excitement of hunting will need to be cherished and nurtured; the dog may be so fired with enthusiasm as you cast it out it may go a little wild. You must take care: use your voice to steady the dog, and keep calm, helping the dog to acknowledge that you are in control, but not inhibiting its intent to concentrate by over-handling or too much whistle-work!

Learn to become aware from which direction the wind is coming. Is it on your back? On your cheek? On your face? Try throwing up a few pieces of grass or straw or hold up a handkerchief in order to familiarise yourself with wind directions, so that eventually it becomes second nature to sense and feel the slightest breath of wind when you are with your dog. You will soon learn that your dog acknowledges which way the breeze is wafting, wherever it is, but what you will not and cannot experience is the scent the dog receives and interprets; in this instance the dog will be the teacher.

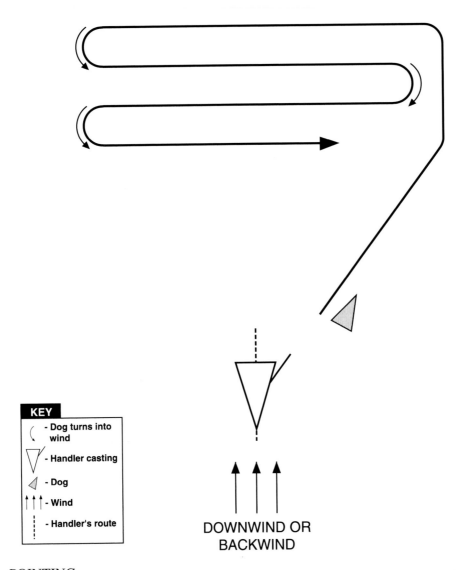

KEY

(- Dog turns into wind

▽ - Handler casting

◁ - Dog

↑↑↑ - Wind

┊ - Handler's route

DOWNWIND OR
BACKWIND

POINTING

Pointers point naturally, it is an instinct. A puppy may start by pointing anything from butterflies to robins, but as the dog matures, it learns to discriminate by scent. It learns to point only live game. When you see your puppy stealthily point, as it stiffens, go to its side quietly, soothe it and stroke its back saying "Steady", encouraging it to stay on point. Move on the object if you can, and make the pup sit so that it may watch its quarry go off. In this way it is learning "Sitting to Flush" as a reflex; but remember, it is all playing at this stage.

Pointing must be one of the most thrilling and amazing sights for a handler to experience – to see your Vizsla in this statuesque trance-like frozen pose and to be able to trust the dog so

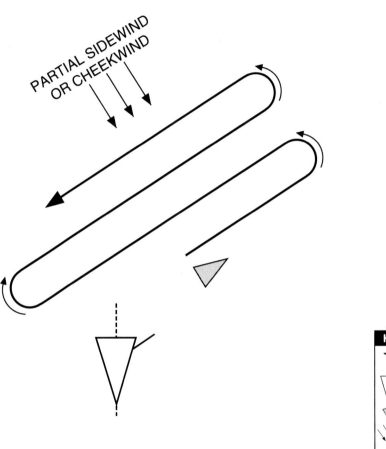

KEY

↱ - Dog turns into wind

▽ - Handler casting

▽ - Dog

\\\ - Wind

⋮ - Handler's route

thoroughly that, although the quarry is hidden, the dog is able to indicate that game is present. The dog may have given the clue before coming on point by the movement of its tail, wagging violently, fast and quick. Suddenly the dog freezes, its body lengthens, its head low, its tail horizontal and stiff; it is mesmerised. Or the dog may come upon scent suddenly within a few feet of a bird; the dog may twist around, its body doubled up in a most tortuous position, to get its nose right there! Until commanded, or the bird moves on, it will remain 'On Point'. This instinct is so powerful and so wonderful to see – it brings the handler into the dog's private, instinctive world.

There is a silly sort of a point, that novice dogs may offer; it's more: "I think there might be, no there isn't." The dog is half-pointing with front foot up, but a languid interest. False

The American style: DC AFC Futaki's Rilenhall Reaghan on point. Owned by Chauncey Smith.

The British style: F.T. Ch. Viszony Of Valotta on point on the grouse moors.

'Tibor' and 'Max' on point. A dog is said to 'back' when it voluntarily adopts a pointing attitude at the sight of another dog on point – a dramatic sight. O'Connell.

pointing is erratic, a haphazard pointing of scents and objects that are unimportant. There are also occasions when a dog may point and advance firmly where birds have been and may be running ahead. If in contrast, the dog has its head on the ground, advances, then slows down, and potters, it may be picking up old scent or a rabbit trail. If your Vizsla has had too much training on dummies it may form a habit of ground-scenting. A youngster used to scenting game early on will hold its head high, accustomed to catching every nuance on the breeze.

AIM: Initially the aim is to control your Vizsla once it has come on point, so that it holds the game until you are able to get up to it from the side. Walk up from behind, taking care not to spoil the dog's point by walking across the ground containing game. Then on your command "Get On", the dog must be encouraged to flush. Eventually your Vizsla will, at times, point and flush at a distance or out of sight without running in.

Now that your youngster is capable of hunting keenly, it can combine quartering with pointing and eventually flushing. It can then finally flush, drop to shot and retrieve. This will be the schedule, but how long it may take to synchronise hunting, pointing and retrieving, will vary from Vizsla to Vizsla; some aspects will be absorbed more easily than others.

The dog must move off point, startling the bird to flight, and remain steady. Szajani Csipke. Owned and bred by S. Harris.   *S. Hart.*

The complete sequence demonstrated by Col. C. Craigie Halkett's 'Trick' on the Aberdeenshire Grouse moors.

The Vizsla confirms the presence of birds – a classic point

The natural progression is:

1. Quarters, points, drops to your flush. Continues quartering.
2. Quarters, points, drops to your flush and shot fired. Continues quartering.
3. Quarters, points, flushes, drops and shot fired, no retrieve.
4. Quarters, points, flushes, drops, shot fired and retrieve.

But first you must go slowly, however excited you are – and you will be. All your infinite patience will come to fruition as long as your Vizsla has had good grounding.

METHOD When you take your Vizsla on to ground with live game, it will be learning to hunt and point on the real thing, and you will be dealing with the dog's natural maturing instincts. At first there should not be any ground game, the reason being that the dog must search for air-borne scent with its nose. If the only scent available is ground scent, i.e. from rabbit or hare, the dog will hunt with its head down with no incentive to raise it.

Initially quarter your dog; when it comes on point, go up to it, soothing to steady; as you push the bird up with your foot, command the dog to drop. Make the dog continue quartering. You can introduce shot at this point, providing you are satisfied that the dog is

Advancing to flush (roading) should be smooth and continuous.

listening to you. At the next stage when the dog is on point, urge it on to flush the bird. It must move in, startling the bird to flight. At first your youngster may get a shock by the violence of a big old cock bird noisily bursting into the air; it may sit automatically. On the other hand, the dog may tend to be sticky on point, refusing to move forward when urged. Reluctance to flush game means that the dog is not producing game for the gun, which is what it is there for. To help the dog over this, the handler must encourage it to move in. Stamping your foot will help move the game on. If the dog is encouraged to flush its own game too early, it may become unsteady. However, the dog should become more reliable, putting its nose under the game to flush it quite naturally. When you finally feel your Vizsla is getting the idea, you can introduce the whole sequence, with less and less human interference, and eventually, the dog may be allowed to retrieve a bird it has pointed, flushed and marked the fall.

Although, classically, you will commence your advanced training on open ground which holds game, where the dog will learn 'Ground Treatment', it will, at times, in Britain, be just as likely to have to deal with thick patches of cover, woodland and dense hedgerows, ditches and roots, when the dog is shot over. The thick undergrowth in wooded areas requires more Spaniel-type work, when the dog needs to burrow its way through in order to push birds out.

The departure of the flushed covey.

Steadiness to gunshot and marking the fall.

Retrieving game, illustrated by Ch. Cuzco Laski, also on the grouse moors.

With experience your Vizsla will learn to move a bird along, and push it up for the guns. Hunting the hedgerows needs a dog which can detect the wind and use it to advantage, knows which way the scent will play, and can, if necessary, work up the opposite side of the hedge to the handler out of sight. This is the time your dog's steadiness is really put to the test. Roots are yet another type of cover; the foliage can be too tall and abundant, birds tend to run on and ahead. The dog's skill will be to 'road' or move forward from the point, to raise the hidden birds, nudging them up into flight – very tempting for a quick snap and a mouthful of feathers. In close type of cover, when there may be many birds, your Vizsla may become besotted with scent and unable to concentrate. You will need to urge the dog to move on constantly. As the dog matures it will learn to produce birds for the guns, and that is what it is there for.

So, as you see, both you and your Vizsla have come a long way in your training, and now it will be put to the test. After a couple of seasons in the field you will realise that the dog is becoming 'field wise'. The aim should be to take every opportunity to increase your youngster's experience – there is no substitute. The dog can be introduced to new forms of shooting ground and all types of game, so that it becomes a genuine, all-round hunting Vizsla. Do not expect your dog to take to it all; there are bound to be difficulties. Your Vizsla is going to be confronted with strange dogs, strange people and strange places, but as long as it has been brought up with the familiar rough and tumble of being with other dogs, and the general experience of fun and laughter, noise, excitement and tension, it will not be worried by much. It is essential that your dog is neither a whiner nor a fighter: both are unacceptable in a gundog, for your dog has to mix with all breeds of gundog and get on with them. It must also get used to being silent while sitting at its post during a drive. Birds flying, guns firing, beaters shouting, rabbits rushing past; understandably such enticements will excite your dog, and inevitably gundogs will rampage at times. But if your dog chases or runs in once in a while, you have the knowledge and ability to deal with the problem. You can always go back to basics and give your dog a refresher course.

I hope during the course of your training you will have sought to join others with whom you can share your efforts to train your Vizsla. By sharing your experiences, problems and achievements, many a pitfall can be avoided. In Britain the requirement for ultimate steadiness in field trialling can be our undoing in training the Vizsla. To achieve the fine edge with a dog, we ask it to be so acutely attuned to its handler, so acutely disciplined, that if asked to drop on a sixpence it must; but it must also be of such independent spirit as to respond to its own innate instincts.

Chapter Twelve

FINAL THOUGHTS

It is wise to attend the hunt, point and retrieve sessions, rather than those organised solely for Retrievers and Spaniels. These classes can be used as a means to an end, dogs and owners having a yardstick against others. The training sessions should cover basic obedience, hunting and pointing, and retrieving. Working Tests are valuable in assessing the success of your dog's training, and can therefore be the outcome of your training classes, and a debut to the shooting field and field trialling. But sooner or later your dog needs to experience more than retrieving dummies. Care must be taken that your Vizsla does not only respond to your commands, but has the opportunity to follow its own instincts as well. There is no substitute for suitable ground where there is a supply of birds, and this is essential if you want to train your Vizsla to work to its full capacity.

Lord Joicey, Hon. Life Member of the H.V. Society, eminent field trial judge, who knows the HPR breeds well, writes: "I fear there is too much emphasis over the years on ultra steadiness. Handlers and judges are obsessed with steadiness and forget that all dogs will make mistakes at some time, even good ones, and with a small group like ours, it is sad to banish good dogs for minor errors – so few seem to know what a good game finder should look like!"

A few years back, I was given advice by a wise old trainer of gundogs. His counsel at the time seemed radical, but I have learned, as many others who work their Vizslas have come to realise through their own experience, that there is much to be said for his radical methods. For the Vizsla who is not to be trialled but used for your own personal hunting, his recommendation was, in certain circumstances, that once your Vizsla was hunting hard, you could go ahead with obedience. But the dog must not be taught to heel or given too many obedience commands until it is hunting hard in the field, otherwise you may find the dog is with you, it is not wanting to hunt, but is waiting to follow commands. It is also recommended that a young dog should not be discouraged from chasing birds at first, as this is good for developing instincts. Then, when the dog's training is well underway, it can be discouraged from chasing.

Louise Petrie Hay (Waidman prefix), field trial judge of the HPRs, Hon. F.T. Secretary of the H.V. Society, and one of the first pioneers of the breed, has always trained and worked Vizslas; she states that the Vizsla's temperament is an anomaly, utterly contradictory. Happiness, confidence and a deep and sincere wish to please are all evident and genuine. Nevertheless, this breed is also sensitive and contrary, soft and very strong-willed. This creates a strange and difficult mixture for training, but for those who understand the dog's character, it is utterly fascinating. The Vizsla's need for physical affection is strong, and more ground can be covered in training by praise than any other method.

Chauncey Smith finds his methods successfully deal with the Vizsla's "strange and difficult mixture" for training:

"I start my puppies in the field very young, at three to four months. If the weather conditions are right, I allow my puppies to follow the older dogs. As far as I am concerned, a young puppy can do no wrong. A lot of people who have visited me over the years, from England and overseas, are shocked at the freedom I give my young dogs. I feel that if you do not let the young Vizsla develop its natural instincts and a little independence, you end up with a dog who does not want to hunt on its own. So, free-style hunting with a young dog is the best thing we can do. I am also a firm believer that too much obedience training with a young dog cuts a lot of its style and desire.

"As the puppies develop their legs at six to nine months, I will let them point, bust, chase, and do whatever they darn well please – in other words, they have a ball! I have seen lots of dogs that are steady to wing and shot, find birds and point birds – or stumble upon a bird and point it. There is a difference between finding a bird and pointing it, and stumbling on a bird and pointing it. Quite a few dogs do not really know how to hunt, and I think part of the reason is that they have not had the opportunity for free-hunting when young.

"At this time I introduce the dogs to birds and to the gun. You must be assured that I do not neglect the basic 'yard-work'. By this I mean basic obedience commands such as "Come", "Stay", "Whoa". This is not done in the field, it is done in the house, out of the house, getting in and out of the car and the kennel. Basic commands have to do with daily life – and the dog does not associate them with birds. I also do retrieving at a young age. I have never been a fan of teaching a pointing dog to sit; I like my dogs to stop and stand. This is all I need at this stage of the game.

"When the dog is twelve months of age or slightly older, exposure in the field is lengthened. When I find my young dog standing on point, the dog is telling me that it is time to start to steady it on birds. If I have done my yard-work properly – in and out of the house, in and out of the kennel, in and out of everywhere – I put a check cord (long rope) on the dog. Then, after commanding the dog to "Stay", I can correct it by yanking the rope if it busts a bird, refuses to back or breaks on shot. (It is helpful to have someone assisting you when doing this work.) The dog then gets the idea it is being punished for disobeying me, not for trying to get the bird.

"In the AKC Field Trials, in order to obtain a win, a dog must be steady to wing (flush) and shot, and retrieve to hand (as in Britain). The dog must also back (honour another dog's point), and as the backing dog it must stand steady to wing and shot, and watch its brace-mate retrieve a bird. In the breaking process, once I know my dog will retrieve a bird, I do not allow it to retrieve every bird I shoot. On some occasions I shoot a bird, walk over, and pick it up myself while my dog is standing. I am trying to develop a question in the dog's mind: "Is he going to get the bird this time, or am I?"

If the end result is that our Vizsla hunts out, produces birds and is ultimately steady enough for our needs, it is always well worth tempering our methods to obtain a final result. The crux of the matter is that the right handler and the right dog can achieve all things. Each dog's temperament is so different, its talents so varied, excelling in one aspect perhaps more than another, that although the principles of training HPRs must be understood and valued, they must be honed and refined according to the individual's needs. A slight leeway should always be allowed; and so, together, the giving and taking result in the sort of Vizsla you want. It has been my aim to show the Vizsla's versatility when properly nurtured and trained, and with due attention to extending its gifts and talents the owner is assured of a most endearing and capable companion. I hope the day never comes when the Vizsla is used soley as a competitive dog, an automaton in the show ring or in the field. Its elements are as a working gundog and a cherished member of the family, where all its qualities can enrich our lives.